JHELLS

Criminal Law

(SECOND EDITION)

Round Hall's Nutshell, Nutcase and Exam Focus Series

NUTSHELL TITLES

Specially written for students of Irish law, each title in the Nutshell series from Round Hall is an accessible review of key principles, concepts and cases. Nutshells are both the ideal introductory text, and the perfect revision aid.

- **NEW – The Irish Legal System by Dorothy Donovan**
- Tort – 2nd edition by Ursula Connolly
- Company Law – 2nd edition by Catherine McConville
- Constitutional Law – 2nd edition by Fergus Ryan
- Land Law by Ruth Cannon
- Contract Law by Fergus Ryan
- Equity Law by Karl Dowling
- Family Law by Louise Crowley
- Employment Law by Dorothy Donovan
- Evidence by Ross Gorman

NUTCASE TITLES

Round Hall Nutcases are written to give you the key facts and principles of **important cases** in core legal subject areas. Straightforward, no-nonsense language makes Nutcases an easy way to understand and learn key cases.

- Tort – 2nd edition by Val Corbett
- Criminal Law by Majella Walsh
- Evidence by Neil Van Dokkum

EXAM FOCUS TITLES

The series is especially designed to support students in the weeks coming up to exams by providing a unique tutorial approach to answering questions.

- Criminal Law by Sarah Carew

NUTSHELLS

Criminal Law

(SECOND EDITION)

by

CECILIA NÍ CHOILEÁIN

BA (NUI), LLB (NUI),
LLM (Trinity College, Dublin)
BL (King's Inns)

ROUND HALL 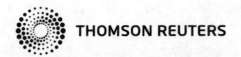 THOMSON REUTERS

Published in 2010 by
Thomson Reuters (Professional) Ireland Limited
(Registered in Ireland, Company No. 80867. Registered Office
and address for service 43 Fitzwilliam Place, Dublin 2)
trading as Round Hall

Typeset by Carrigboy Typesetting Services

Printed by ColourBooks, Dublin

ISBN 978–1–85800–595–9

A catalogue record for this book is available from the British Library.

"Do mo theaghlach, Betty, Seán Cathal agus John, le meas, mile buíochas agus grá."

"Í gcuimhne ar Sandra agus Caroline."

Acknowledgements

There are a number of people to whom I owe a debt of gratitude for their help with this book. In particular, I'd like to thank all at Thomson Reuters and especially Frieda Donohue and Kristiina Kojamo for their courtesy, patience and unfailing good humour. I am grateful to my colleagues, past and present, for their help with both editions of this book. Finally, I'd like to thank my family and friends, and in particular, Hilary Band.

Biography

Cecilia Ní Choileáin BA (Hons)(NUI), LLB (Hons)(NUI), LLM (Hons) (Trinity College, Dublin), BL (King's Inns) is a barrister, having been called to the Bar of Ireland in 2005. She is currently a legal researcher in the Library and Research Service of the Houses of the Oireachtas. She has tutored in Employment Law and the Sociology of Law in the Law Faculty, NUI, Galway and is a former lecturer in Constitutional Law in the Dublin Institute of Technology, where she also tutored in Criminal Law. She is a former researcher in the Judicial Researchers' Office, Four Courts, Dublin and in the Office of the Parliamentary Legal Advisor to the Houses of the Oireachtas.

Contents

Table of Cases

ENGLAND

CRIMINAL LAW

NORTHERN IRELAND

AUSTRALIA

Table of Legislation

Irish Statutes

ENGLISH STATUTES

ENGLISH STATUTORY INSTRUMENTS

OTHER

Introduction

It is impossible in a book of this nature to cover all aspects of an area of law as broad and diverse as the criminal law in any great depth. Its objective, then, is to set out the most fundamental principles of criminal law as they operate in this jurisdiction, and to update the previous edition of this book in light of subsequent changes in the law.

Before looking at the substantive areas covered by the criminal law which are contained in subsequent chapters, a few general points need to be made about the criminal law itself and its function in this, or indeed any, society.

THE FUNCTION OF THE CRIMINAL LAW

The behaviour of individuals in any society is subject to regulation in a number of ways. Social norms and customs, religion and the laws of any jurisdiction are just some of the methods through which the behaviour of human beings can be curtailed in an attempt to establish and maintain a peaceful and ordered society. Of all these methods, criminal law is unique in that it is the only method of social control which is enforced by means of state-imposed sanctions on the transgressing individual. The criminal law of any jurisdiction sets out the various types of behaviour which are deemed to be unacceptable to the members of that society, and which are considered to be sufficiently serious to warrant the involvement of the State. Unlike other areas of law, such as the law of contract and the law of tort, both of which involve disputes between private individuals, criminal law is an area of public law in which the individual against whom allegations of criminal activity are made is prosecuted by the State in the name of the people. Upon conviction, the offender will be subject to court-imposed sanctions which are prescribed by law and enforced by the executive.

In this jurisdiction, criminal activity is that which is expressly prohibited by statute. In addition, there are numerous offences recognised by the common law and a very small number which are provided for by Bunreacht na hÉireann. Regardless of the source of the offence, all remain subject to the requirements of Bunreacht na hÉireann which imposes a number of obligations on the State in respect of individual rights. Society's interest in the suppression of criminal activity and the effective operation of its criminal justice system requires a coherent body of rules, an impartial and independent judiciary, and an adequately resourced and trained police force. On the other hand, the seriousness of the consequences to the individual charged with a criminal offence requires that at all stages, from the investigation of an offence through to the outcome of a criminal trial, the individual is possessed of numerous rights provided for by law. Anyone charged with a criminal offence in this jurisdiction is entitled by law to be presumed innocent until the contrary be proven beyond a reasonable doubt before an impartial judge and, subject to certain exceptions, a jury. While it will normally be in society's interests to prosecute criminal activity, there are instances in which this interest must yield to a greater interest in protecting the individual. The clearest example of this occurs where the accused person is deemed not fit to stand trial, in accordance with the provisions of the Criminal Law (Insanity) Act 2006. In addition, there are various defences available to the individual charged with a criminal offence. These can operate in such a way as to either excuse or justify the behaviour of the defendant. The right of an accused person to be presumed innocent places the burden of proof on the prosecution, who must not only prove all the elements of the charge(s) against the accused, beyond a reasonable doubt, but also negative any defence(s) and/or explanations put forward by the defence which are consistent with the innocence of the accused.

Sources of Criminal Law

The primary sources of Irish criminal law are legislation and the common law, both of which will be discussed briefly. The role played by Bunreacht na hÉireann is of fundamental importance, since it provides the framework within which the criminal law must operate. Like other areas of law, the criminal law may be said to come from different sources. These are mainly legislation/ statute and the common law.

STATUTE

As provided for by Bunreacht na hÉireann, sole legislative power is vested in the Oireachtas, with the caveat that any legislation enacted must comply with constitutional requirements such as the prohibition on the enactment of legislation which is retrospective in effect and that which is unconstitutional by virtue of its incompatibility with any of the provisions of Bunreacht na hÉireann. Criminal statutes may be enacted to create entirely new offences, to codify existing common law rules or to add to existing common law offences.

COMMON LAW

Since the enactment of Bunreacht na hÉireann with its prohibition on law-making by any body other than the Oireachtas, judges have not been able to declare acts to be illegal as they had been able to for centuries. Nevertheless, the common law remains a very important legal resource in that many of the rules and principles which are employed by the courts have been created by the common law courts. The decisions of courts in other common law jurisdictions, although not binding on Irish courts, are of persuasive value. At common law, offences were categorised as treasons, felonies and mis-demeanours, the first two types being the most serious and the latter being less grave in nature. The distinction between felonies and misdemeanours was abolished in this jurisdiction by s.3 of the Criminal Law Act 1997, which replaced the category of felonies with a new classification of offences, known as arrestable offences. An arrestable offence is defined as one which carries a potential sentence of five years or more. Offences are also categorised as "indictable" or "summary". Indictable offences are tried on indictment in the Circuit, Central or Special Criminal Courts or in some cases in the District Court if the offence in question is an "either-or" offence, subject to the conditions outlined in the paragraph relating to the criminal jurisdiction of the District Court. Summary offences are less serious in nature and are dealt with in the District Court.

THE IMPACT OF BUNREACHT NA HÉIREANN 1937

Bunreacht na hÉireann 1937 is the primary source of law in this jurisdiction. A number of articles of Bunreacht na hÉireann are of particular relevance to the criminal law. The following is a brief outline of those:

Article 15.2.1 vests sole law-making power in the Oireachtas. Due to the operation of the doctrine of the Separation of Powers, no other body, including the judicial arm of the State, has the power to make law.

Article 15.4.1 precludes the Oireachtas from enacting any law that is repugnant to any part of Bunreacht na hÉireann.

Article 15.5 forbids the enactment of any legislation that is retrospective in its effect. This is in keeping with the maxim *nullem crimen sine lege, nulla poena sine lege* which translates as "no crime without law, no punishment without law".

Article 15.13 provides immunity from arrest for criminal offences except treason, felony (now abolished) and breach of the peace for any member of either House of Oireachtas, going to, coming from or while within the precincts of either House of the Oireachtas.

Article 26 provides for the procedure by which the President may, after consultation with the Council of State, refer a Bill to the Supreme Court for a determination as to its constitutionality. If a Bill survives a challenge under the Article, it must be signed into law by the President and is immune from further challenge.

Article 30.1 provides for the office of the Attorney General who is the legal advisor to the Government.

Article 30.3 provides that all crimes other than summary offences shall be prosecuted in the name of the People and at the suit of the Attorney General "or some other person authorised in accordance with law to act for that purpose". Since the establishment of the office of the Director of Public Prosecutions pursuant to the provisions of the Prosecution of Offences Act 1974, the vast majority of prosecutions are taken by the DPP although there appears to be nothing to stop the Attorney General from prosecuting any non-summary offence and there are a small number of offences that may only be prosecuted by the Attorney General.

Article 34 and its subsections relate to the courts. Provision is made for the establishment of Courts of First Instance and a Court of Final Appeal. Under Art.34, the High Court is vested with "full original jurisdiction in and power to determine all matters and questions whether of law or fact, civil or criminal".

Article 34.3.2 is of particular importance in that it provides that only the High Court has jurisdiction to determine the constitutionality of any law, subject to an appeal to the Supreme Court.

Article 35 relates to the appointment and tenure of judges.

Article 37 provides that limited powers of a judicial nature may be exercised by a person or body of persons other than a judge or a court. Criminal matters are expressly *excluded* from this, which means that no person or body of persons other than a judge or a court can determine matters of a criminal nature.

Article 38 deals with the Trial of Offences and provides, in subs.(1) that, "no person shall be tried on any criminal charge save in due course of law".

Article 38.2 states that minor offences may be tried by courts of summary jurisdiction.

Article 38.3.1 declares that, "special courts may be established by law for the trial of offences in cases where it may be determined in accordance with such law that the ordinary courts are inadequate to secure the effective administration of justice, and the preservation of public peace and order". The Special Criminal Court was set up under the Offences Against the State Act 1939 pursuant to the terms of this Article and its subsections.

Article 38.5 provides that, "save in the case of the trial of offences under Section 2, Section 3 or Section 4 of this Article, no person shall be tried on any criminal charge without a jury". This means that summary trials (Art.38.2), trials in the Special Criminal Court (Art.38.3) and trials before Military Tribunals (Art.38.4) are not required to be held before a jury and that the trial of an accused person in these circumstances is not unconstitutional by virtue of the absence of a jury.

Articles 40–44 deal with fundamental and personal rights. Many of these are enumerated such as personal liberty (Art.40.1), and Freedom of Assembly (Art.40.6.1(ii)). Others are unenumerated but are no less significant. Examples of unenumerated personal rights include:

- Privacy—held in *Kennedy v Ireland* [1987] I.R. 587.
- Bodily integrity—held in *Ryan v AG* [1965] I.R. 294.
- Free legal aid in criminal cases—held in *The State (Healy) v Donoghue* [1976] I.R. 325.

Article 40.4 provides for the procedure known as habeas corpus whereby a person may question the legality of his detention.

Article 50 provides that laws in force in Saorstát Éireann immediately prior to the enactment of Bunreacht na hÉireann will be deemed to have been "carried over" into the law of the new State provided that they are not inconsistent with the provisions of Bunreacht na hÉireann and that they have not been repealed. Any statutory provision or rule of common law that preceded the enactment of Bunreacht na hÉireann are challenged under Art.50, the most recent example of which was the challenge to s.1(1) of the Criminal Law Amendment Act 1935 which was deemed to be unconstitutional in *CC v Ireland and the Attorney General* [2006] 4 I.R. 1.

In the context of the criminal law, two important factors should be noted.

(1) Breaches of the constitutional rights of an accused person may well lead to an arrest, detention, prosecution or trial being invalid. It must be said, however, that no right is absolute and even a constitutionally protected right may have to give way to a superior right or interest on occasion. *The People (DPP) v Shaw* [1982] I.R. 1 is one such example. In this case a confession obtained at a time when the accused was being detained unconstitutionally was nevertheless admitted into evidence on the basis that the Gardaí had breached his constitutional right to liberty in order to vindicate the right to life of a woman who had been kidnapped by the accused. Unknown to Gardaí, the woman had, in fact been murdered by the accused. In this case, it was held that the woman's right to life took precedence over the accused's right to liberty and the evidence was allowed.

(2) Legislation or rules of common law can be challenged using the process known as judicial review. The net effect of a finding of unconstitutionality is that the legislation or common law rule in question is of no legal consequence. Different considerations apply depending on the vintage of the impugned law. If the legislation or rule of common law predates the enactment of Bunreacht na hÉireann, the question for the court will be whether it was "carried over" into the law of the modern Irish State in accordance with Art.50. Such laws do not enjoy any presumption of constitutionality and if they are found to be repugnant to the terms of

Bunreacht na hÉireann, are deemed not to have been carried over and never to have been valid in this jurisdiction. See, for example, the decision of the Supreme Court in *CC v Ireland and the Attorney General* referred to above.

Where the impugned law was passed after the enactment of Bunreacht na hÉireann, it is reviewed under Art.34. Any law passed since 1937 is presumed to be constitutional. Where such a law is then found to be unconstitutional it is declared to have been void ab initio, in other words, it was never valid. Bills are also presumed to be constitutional unless/until they are challenged under Art.26 of Bunreacht na hÉireann. Only the President may refer a Bill to the Supreme Court for a ruling as to its constitutionality and this reference may only be made following a consultation by the President with the Council of State. A Bill that survives a challenge under Art.26 is then immune from further challenge, even if constitutional rights are subsequently infringed by it. In *Re Ó Laighléis* [1960] I.R. 93 the plaintiff had been interned without trial pursuant to the provisions of the Offences Against the State (Amendment) Act 1940. He challenged the Act on the basis that it infringed his constitutional rights. However, the Act had been passed following an unsuccessful Article 26 challenge in *Re Article 26 and the Offences Against the State (Amendment) Bill, 1940* [1940] I.R. 470 and was therefore immune from further challenge.

THE EUROPEAN CONVENTION ON HUMAN RIGHTS

Prior to the incorporation of the European Convention on Human Rights (the "Convention") into domestic law by the European Convention on Human Rights Act 2003, Ireland did have international obligations under the Convention, and was amenable to the jurisdiction of the European Court of Human Rights. This, however, did not mean that the Convention could be invoked before the Irish courts due to the fact that while the Convention was binding upon the State, it was not binding within it. Consequently, an individual who alleged that his rights under the Convention had been breached had to take his case to the European Court of Human Rights in Strasbourg in order to have the right in question vindicated.

THE EUROPEAN CONVENTION ON HUMAN RIGHTS ACT 2003

Having opted to incorporate the ECHR into domestic law at sub-constitutional level, the legislature has ensured that the status of the Constitution remains the same. However, s.2(1) of the Act provides that, "in interpreting and applying any statutory provision or rule of law, a court shall, in so far as is possible, subject to the rules of law relating to such interpretation and application, do so in a manner compatible with the State's obligations under the Convention provisions". The Act requires that judicial notice must be taken of all decisions and declarations of the European Court of Human Rights and that the courts interpret legislation "in so far as is possible" in conformity with the provisions of the Convention. This is likely to mean that the courts will continue to interpret legislation in conformity with the provisions of Bunreacht na hÉireann even where this might mean that to do so would not be in keeping with the terms of the ECHR. This will mean that applicants will still have to go to Strasbourg to let the European Court of Human Rights adjudicate on the matter. The European Court of Human Rights may only exercise its jurisdiction in cases where domestic remedies have been exhausted and an application to the European Court of Human Rights must be made within six months of the decision under challenge. The High Court and the Supreme Court on appeal may declare that a statutory provision or a rule of law violates the Convention but neither court is empowered to strike the offending legislation or rule of law down solely on this basis. The only obligation imposed by the Act is that where a rule of law or statutory provision is declared by a court to be incompatible with the terms of the Convention, the Taoiseach must cause a statement to be made in both Houses of the Oireachtas to that effect. The Oireachtas is not obliged to enact legislation that will accord with the provisions of the Convention, which could mean that legislation which is deemed to be incompatible with the Convention will remain on the books, although it will still be open to an aggrieved individual to pursue the matter before the European Court of Human Rights. Provision is made in the Act for an ex gratia payment to be made by the Government to a party who has suffered loss, damage or injury as a result of the violation of the Convention where an application has been made in this regard by the aggrieved party to the Attorney General. In the context of criminal law the most important rights covered by the Convention are:

- Life (Art.2);
- Freedom from torture/inhuman/degrading treatment (Art.3);
- Liberty (Art.5);
- Fair trial (Art.6);
- Non-retrospectivity in criminal law legislation (Art.7);
- Expression (Art.8); and
- Freedom of peaceful assembly (Art.11).

The Jurisdiction of the Irish Courts in Criminal Matters

THE DISTRICT COURT

The country is divided into 24 districts, the Dublin Metropolitan District and 23 others outside Dublin. The 23 districts outside Dublin are sub-divided into numerous smaller districts, each with its own sitting of the District Court. Each District Court is a court of local and limited jurisdiction and in the context of criminal offences is a court of summary jurisdiction. The court is presided over by a judge who sits without a jury. Article 38.2 of Bunreacht na hÉireann provides that minor offences may be tried summarily although it is silent on the issue of what constitutes a minor offence.

In *Melling v Ó Mathghamhna* [1962] I.R. 1, the Supreme Court stated that when deciding whether an offence was minor, regard should be had to two factors:

(1)   the severity of the punishment attracted by the offence, and
(2)   the nature of the offence itself.

See also *Conroy v Attorney General* [1965] I.R. 411.

Where an offence is provided for by statute, it will indicate whether an offence is one capable of being tried summarily.

The District Court is a court of limited and summary jurisdiction, and may deal with:

(i)   Cases in the district court area in which the alleged offence was committed;
(ii)   Cases in the area where the defendant lives or carries out business;
(iii) Cases in the area in which the defendant was arrested;
(iv)   Certain offences, contained in the Schedule to the Criminal Justice Act 1951 may be tried on indictment or summarily in the District Court, provided that:
(1)   The District Court judge accepts jurisdiction.
(2)   The accused consents to the offence being tried summarily, bearing in mind that he will forego his right to be tried by a jury.

(3) The consent of the Director of Public Prosecutions may also be required for the summary disposal of the offence in question.
(v) Indictable offences which are triable summarily.

Indictable offences will also be sent forward by the District Court for trial upon service of the Book of Evidence.

THE CIRCUIT COURT

The country is divided into eight circuits, each Circuit Court being a court of local and limited jurisdiction. The Circuit Court has jurisdiction to try all indictable offences with the exception of those which can only be tried before the Central Criminal Court. In addition to its first instance jurisdiction with regard to most indictable offences, the Circuit Court has appellate jurisdiction of decisions of the District Court. An appeal against conviction in the District Court may be made to the Circuit Court. The matter is then dealt with *de novo* by the Circuit Court and no appeal lies from that decision.
    This court sits with a judge and jury and may deal with:

   (i) Cases in the circuit court area in which the alleged offence was committed;
  (ii) Cases in the area where the defendant lives or carries out business;
 (iii) Cases in the area in which the defendant was arrested; and
  (iv) Cases may be transferred from one part of a circuit to another. Where the Director of Public Prosecutions or the accused applies for a transfer of a case, the Circuit Court judge may, if satisfied that it would be manifestly unfair not to do so, transfer a trial from the circuit court sitting outside Dublin to the Dublin Circuit Court.

The court has jurisdiction to try all non-minor offences except murder, rape, aggravated sexual assault, treason, piracy and related offences.

THE HIGH COURT/THE CENTRAL CRIMINAL COURT

Article 34.3.1 of Bunreacht na hÉireann provides that the High Court has "full jurisdiction in and power to determine all matters and questions whether of law or fact, civil or criminal".
    The High Court, when exercising its criminal jurisdiction, is known as the Central Criminal Court. The court is presided over by a judge sitting with a jury.

The court deals with those criminal offences which are outside the jurisdiction of the Circuit Court. These are:

- murder, attempted murder, conspiracy to murder;
- treason—defined in Art.39 of Bunreacht na hÉireann and provided for by the Treason Act 1939;
- piracy;
- certain offences under the Offences Against the State Acts 1939–1998;
- rape, aggravated sexual assault and attempted aggravated sexual assault; and
- offences against the Genocide Act 1973, the Geneva Conventions Act 1962 and the Criminal Justice (United Nations Conventions Against Torture) Act 2000.

The High Court has jurisdiction to deal with questions sent to it on a "case stated" basis. Where the District Court refers a matter to the High Court while a case is ongoing, the procedure is referred to as a "consultative case stated".

THE SPECIAL CRIMINAL COURT

This court was set up under Pt V of the Offences Against the State Act 1939 and is one of the constitutionally permissible instances in which an accused person may be tried without a jury. The constitutional basis for the court is to be found in Art.38.3 which provides that, "Special Courts may be established by law for the trial of offences in cases where it may be determined in accordance with such law that the ordinary courts are inadequate to secure the effective administration of justice, and the preservation of public peace and order". The Special Criminal Court sits with three judges and no jury.

Offences contained in the Schedule to the Offences Against the State Act 1939 are dealt with by the Special Criminal Court as are offences in respect of which the Director of Public Prosecutions has issued a certificate declaring that in his opinion, the ordinary courts are inadequate to secure the administration of justice. The Criminal Justice (Amendment) Act 2009 creates a number of new offences pertaining to criminal organisations. The jurisdiction of the Special Criminal Court has been extended to include these offences. In effect, therefore, any serious offence can come before the Special Criminal Court, even those which have no "subversive" element. See, for example *The People (Director of Public Prosecutions) v Quilligan* [1986] I.R. 495. In *Savage v Director of Public Prosecutions* [1982] I.L.R.M. 385, the court stated that the decisions of the Director of Public Prosecutions are generally not amenable to judicial review.

THE COURT OF CRIMINAL APPEAL

The Court of Criminal Appeal sits with three judges and has appellate jurisdiction only. The court can hear appeals against convictions from the Circuit, Central and Special Criminal Courts. Appeals are heard on the basis that the trial judge(s) have granted leave to appeal or where such leave to appeal has been refused, the Court of Criminal Appeal may itself grant leave to appeal. An appeal against conviction is premised on the assertion that the trial judge(s) either erred in law or that the trial was unsatisfactory for some other reason.

In cases involving appeals against conviction, the Court of Criminal Appeal can either:

(a) affirm the conviction;
(b) allow the appeal and order a retrial; or
(c) allow the appeal and enter an acquittal.

The Court of Criminal Appeal also hears appeals against sentence. These appeals can be made by either the convicted person on the basis that the sentence is too harsh or by the prosecution who may appeal against the leniency of the sentence. In either case, the court looks at whether the sentence imposed deviated from the range of sentences usually handed down for that particular offence with regard to the circumstances of the convicted person and of the offence itself.

Both these types of appeals are dealt with on the basis of the transcripts from the trial courts. In cases in which a miscarriage of justice is alleged due to the existence of a newly discovered fact, the court will hear this new evidence. If the court is satisfied that a miscarriage of justice has taken place, it may issue a certificate to that effect which will then result in a payment of compensation for the aggrieved party. In *The People (Director of Public Prosecutions) v Pringle* [1997] 2 I.R. 225, it was held that there was no exhaustive definition of "miscarriage of justice" and that furthermore, no such definition should be attempted. In *The People (Director of Public Prosecutions) v Nora Wall* [2005] IECCA 140, the court gave some examples of situations which could amount to miscarriages of justice but said that the list was not definitive. These examples include: where the innocence of the accused is established; where the prosecution ought not to have been pursued due to a lack of credible evidence; where the trial was conducted in a manner inconsistent with judicial or constitutional procedure; and where, as occurred in *The People (Director of Public Prosecutions) v Frank Shortt (No. 2)* [2002] 2 I.R. 696, there had been a grave defect in the administration of justice brought on by the agents of the State.

THE SUPREME COURT

The Supreme Court is a court of appellate jurisdiction only and has original jurisdiction in only two matters. These are firstly, the determination, pursuant to Art.12 of Bunreacht na hÉireann, as to whether the President has become permanently incapacitated and secondly, the reference made by the President under Art.26 of Bunreacht na hÉireann for a determination as to the constitutionality of a Bill or part thereof. The composition of the court varies depending on the type of proceedings but in general the court comprises three or five judges. Additionally, since the Supreme Court is not a trial court, proceedings are based on transcripts and documentation which had been before the trial court. An appeal lies to the Supreme Court from a decision of the Court of Criminal Appeal where the latter court, the Director of Public Prosecutions or the Attorney General certifies that, "a point of law of exceptional public importance" has arisen from the case in question which requires, in the public interest, a decision of the Supreme Court. See for example:

- *The People (Director of Public Prosecutions v Murray* [1977] I.R. 360
- *The People (Director of Public Prosecutions) v Pringle* [1997] 2 I.R. 225

In addition, the Supreme Court deals with matters referred to it by way of case stated from the Circuit Court and the High Court. A decision of the High Court on a case stated basis from the District Court may be appealed to the Supreme Court.

> **KEY CASES AND LEGISLATION**
>
> *Melling v Ó Mathghamhna* [1962] I.R. 1—Factors determining whether offence is minor.

Arrest and Detention

4

Article 40.4 of Bunreacht na hÉireann provides that, "no citizen shall be deprived of his personal liberty save in accordance with law". Subsequent subsections of the Article lay out the procedure known as habeas corpus which is an investigation into the legality of detention. This chapter sets out the law relating to the arrest and detention of a suspect, and the statutory provisions which prescribe the maximum duration of detention periods. The habeas corpus procedure is also briefly outlined.

ARREST

An arrest at common law was defined by O'Higgins C.J. in *The People (DPP) v Walsh* [1980] I.R. 294 as being "the actual or notional seizure of a person for the purpose of imprisonment".

In *The People (DPP) v McCreesh* [1992] I.L.R.M. 239, the Supreme Court defined an arrest in the following terms:

> "[A]n arrest consists in or involves the seizure or touching of a person's body accompanied by a form of words which indicate to that person that he is under restraint. Whilst the older cases held that words alone would not suffice to constitute an arrest, nowadays words alone may amount to an arrest, if, in the circumstances they are calculated to bring, and do bring, to the person's notice that he is under restraint and he submitted to the compulsion."

A person may generally only be arrested for the purpose of bringing him before a court to be charged with an offence. It is essential that the person is told the true reason for his arrest and the fact that he is under arrest must be clearly communicated to him. An arrest may be carried out pursuant to a warrant or, in some cases, without a warrant pursuant to the Criminal Law Act 1997. There must be a reasonable suspicion, backed up by evidence, that the suspect has committed an offence.

An arrest may be carried out by any person who has reasonable cause to believe that an arrestable offence has been committed or is being committed

CRIMINAL LAW

by the suspect *and* that the person has reasonable cause to believe that the suspect could or attempt to avoid being arrested by An Garda Síochána. An arrestable offence is defined in the Criminal Law Act 1997 as one which carries a maximum sentence of five years' imprisonment or more. This is commonly referred to as a "citizen's arrest" which had been permitted under common law. It is now, however, provided for by s.4 of the Criminal Law Act 1997. In these circumstances, the suspect must be handed over to An Garda Síochána without delay.

Members of An Garda Síochána, unsurprisingly, have wider powers of arrest and may arrest, without warrant, any person whom the member believes, with reasonable cause, has committed an arrestable offence. Additional powers of arrest are granted to An Garda Síochána in respect of many statutory offences such as those provided for by the Road Traffic Acts. The absence of reasonable suspicion that an arrestable offence has been committed will render the arrest invalid and any detention pursuant to that arrest, unlawful. In *The State (Trimbole) v Governor of Mountjoy Prison* [1985] I.R. 306, an arrest was carried out in the absence of any reasonable cause to believe an offence had been committed. Gardaí arrested the individual for the sole purpose of detaining him pending the arrival of an extradition warrant. Due to the fact that there was no other reason to arrest him, his release was ordered on the grounds that his arrest was unlawful.

Members of An Garda Síochána may also, pursuant to s.6 of the Criminal Law Act 1997, enter any premises for the purpose of arresting a suspect on foot of a warrant or order of committal. This permission extends to entry by An Garda Síochána into a dwelling and reasonable force may be used to carry out the arrest, if necessary. The person whose arrest is sought must be on the premises or the member must have reasonable cause to believe that he is on the premises. Where there is no arrest warrant, s.6(2) of the Criminal Law Act 1997 provides that a member of An Garda Síochána may only enter a dwelling with the consent of the occupier or other person who appears to the member to be in charge of the dwelling *and* one of the following criteria is met:

(a) the person to be arrested has been observed within the dwelling or entering the dwelling by the arresting officer or another member of An Garda Síochána;
(b) the arresting officer has reasonable grounds for believing that the person to be arrested will abscond in order to avoid justice or otherwise seek to obstruct the course of justice before an arrest warrant can be obtained;
(c) the arresting officer has reasonable cause to suspect that an arrestable offence would be committed by the person before an arrest warrant can be obtained; or
(d) the person to be arrested ordinarily resides in the dwelling.

Once arrested, the suspect must be brought before the District Court to be charged with the offence, at the earliest practicable opportunity, even if this means that a special sitting of the District Court must be arranged. An exception to this occurs where the suspect is arrested after 5pm. In these situations, it is permissible to hold that person overnight until the court sits the following morning.

There is no general right to arrest for questioning. However, there are some exceptions to this general rule and they are as follows:

(1) Under s.4 of the Criminal Justice Act 1984 (as amended), a suspect may be detained for questioning for an initial period of six hours. This initial period may be extended by another six hours by a Garda of the rank of Superintendent or higher. A further extension of 12 hours is permissible where directed by a Garda not below the rank of Chief Superintendent. The member authorising the extended periods of detention must have reasonable grounds for believing that the continued detention of the suspect is required for the proper investigation of the offence and not merely for questioning. The maximum permissible period of detention under s.4 (as amended) is 24 hours.

(2) Section 30 of the Offences Against the State Act 1939 (as amended), permits the detention of a person arrested on suspicion of an offence "scheduled" to the Act for an initial period of 24 hours. A further period of 24 hours may be granted with the consent of a member of the Gardaí of the rank of Chief Superintendent or higher. Another period of 24 hours may be granted by a District judge. The maximum permissible period of detention under s.30 is therefore 72 hours. The constitutionality of s.30 was upheld by the Supreme Court in *The People (Director of Public Prosecutions) v Quilligan* [1987] I.L.R.M. 606.

(3) Section 2 of the Drug Trafficking Act 1996 allows for a suspect to be detained for an initial period of six hours. Further extensions may be granted as follows:

- A further period of 18 hours may be granted with the consent of a Chief Superintendent.
- Another 24 hour period may subsequently be granted, again with the consent of a Chief Superintendent. A further period of 72 hours may be granted where a District or Circuit Court judge consents. Finally, another period of 48 hours may be granted with the consent of a District or Circuit Court judge. The maximum period of detention under this Act is 168 hours/seven days.

(4) Section 50 of the Criminal Justice Act 2007 also permits the detention of a suspect for up to 168 hours/seven days. The initial period permitted under the Act is six hours. This period may be extended for a further 18 hours on the authorisation of a Superintendent. A second period of extension of up to 24 hours may be granted on the authorisation of a Chief Superintendent. Thereafter, provision is made for applications for two further extensions. These may only be granted on application to the District Court or the Circuit Court. The first extension is for a period not exceeding 72 hours and the second period cannot exceed 48 hours.

RIGHTS ON ARREST AND DURING DETENTION

(1) A suspect has the right to remain silent and to be made aware of that right. This right is seen as a corollary of the right to communicate held in *Attorney General v Paperlink* [1984] I.L.R.M. 373 and that of freedom of expression as provided by Art.40.6.1(i) of Bunreacht na hÉireann and was the ruling of the Supreme Court in *Heaney v Ireland* [1994] 1 I.R. 580.

(2) A suspect must be told why he is being arrested—*The People (Director of Public Prosecutions) v Walsh* [1980] I.R. 294. This does not necessarily mean that the precise provision of the Act in question must be cited to the suspect, but he must be given the reason for his arrest.

(3) A suspect has the right to legal aid if he cannot afford legal representation— *The State (Healy) v Donoghue* [1976] I.R. 325.

(4) A suspect has the right to consult with a lawyer. Failure by the Gardaí to allow for this will render the suspect's detention unlawful—*The People (Director of Public Prosecutions) v Healy* [1990] I.L.R.M. 313. A suspect has the right to privacy in his consultations with his lawyer but does not have the right to:
    (a) be informed of his right to see a lawyer—*The People (Director of Public Prosecutions) v Farrell* [1978] I.R. 336; and
    (b) have his lawyer present during interrogation—*The People (Director of Public Prosecutions) v Pringle* [1981] 2 Frewen 57.

(5) A suspect has the right to food, rest and medical treatment.

(6) A suspect has the right of access to the courts.

A person who wishes to question the validity of his detention may invoke the procedure known as habeas corpus. This procedure involves an inquiry under Art.40.4.2 of Bunreacht na hÉireann and involves an application to the High Court or any judge thereof, by the person detained or by someone on his behalf, for a conditional order compelling the person causing the detention to produce the detainee before the court and to provide the court with justification for the detention. Under the terms of Bunreacht na hÉireann, the matter must be looked into "forthwith". The court must order the release of the detainee if it is not satisfied that the detention is in accordance with the law.

KEY CASES AND LEGISLATION

The People (Director of Public Prosecutions) v Walsh [1980] I.R. 294 and *The People (Director of Public Prosecutions) v McCreesh* [1992] I.L.R.M. 239—Definitions of "arrest".

The State (Trimbole) v Governor of Mountjoy Prison [1985] I.R. 306—Absence of reasonable grounds renders arrest and subsequent detention invalid.

Bail

5

Article 40.4.1 of Bunreacht na hÉireann states that, "no citizen shall be deprived of his personal liberty save in due course of law". The issue of bail arises in two situations. The first of these is where an accused person has been charged with an offence and wishes to be released on bail pending trial. The second of these situations occurs where the accused, having been convicted, wishes to appeal against either his conviction or the sentence imposed by the court and applies to be released on bail until the hearing of his appeal. For the purposes of this chapter, the issue of bail will be dealt with in the context of the former of the two situations, this being the more usual of the two.

Essentially, bail is a form of conditional release, the main condition being that the accused person will turn up to face trial. Bail is granted upon the accused person entering into a recognisance, with or without sureties. What this means is that the accused person agrees to abide by whatever conditions the court may impose, and crucially, that he will show up to face trial. Breach of any bail conditions or failure to attend for his trial by the accused will lead to the issuing of a bench warrant for his arrest and the forfeiture of whatever sum of money has been lodged either by the accused person himself or by a third party on his behalf. He may also be arrested without warrant. The main issue that arises in the context of bail is that of the valid grounds upon which bail may be refused. It must be borne in mind that at this stage, the accused person has not yet been tried for the offence in question, much less convicted of it, and that unless/until he is convicted, he is entitled under the terms of Bunreacht na hÉireann to the presumption of innocence.

JURISDICTION TO GRANT BAIL

Jurisdiction to grant bail is provided for by s.31 of the Criminal Procedure Act 1967, as amended by the Criminal Justice (Miscellaneous Provisions) Act 1997 and more recently by the Criminal Justice Act 2007. This procedure is known as "station bail". The sergeant/member in charge of a Garda station may "if he considers it prudent to do so and no warrant directing the detention of that person is in force, release him on bail and for that purpose take from him a recognisance, with or without sureties, for his due appearance before the District Court at the appropriate time and place".

The jurisdiction of the District Court to grant bail is provided for by s.28 of the Criminal Procedure Act 1967, as amended by the Bail Act 1997. The District Court is obliged to admit an accused person to bail provided that the case is one in which bail should be granted. The decision of the District Court may be appealed to the High Court, which also has jurisdiction to grant bail at first instance. In the case of certain offences, such as murder, piracy and treason, bail may only be granted on application to the High Court.

Admission to bail usually involves the accused and his sureties acknowledging that they are liable to forfeit a sum of money if bail conditions are disobeyed.

VALID GROUNDS FOR REFUSAL OF BAIL

The traditional view had been that if there was a possibility that the accused would commit another offence while on bail, the court would be entitled to take this into account when deciding whether to grant bail. The criteria governing the granting or refusal of bail were laid down by Hanna J. in *The State v Purcell* [1942] I.R. 207. These were:

(a) The seriousness of the charge faced by the accused.
(b) The severity of the punishment imposed by law.
(c) The strength of the case against the accused.
(d) The prospect of a reasonably speedy trial.
(e) The opposition of the Attorney General.

In *Attorney General v Duffy* [1942] I.R. 529, Hanna J. added another criterion to the list, which was that if there was evidence that the accused was likely to interfere with the course of justice, the court would be entitled to consider this as a material ground against bail being granted.

The Supreme Court endorsed the criteria set down by Hanna J. in *Purcell* and *Duffy* in *The People (Attorney General) v Crosbie* [1966] I.R. 426, where Ó'Dálaigh C.J. summed up the position of bail in the following terms:

> "These applicants are charged with non-capital murder and counsel for the Attorney General has given an unqualified 'no' in answer to the Court's question, 'is it apprehended that the applicants will abscond if bailed?' Nor, moreover is it apprehended that there will be any interference with witnesses. In these circumstances it is the Court's duty to admit these untried prisoners to bail."

Ó'Dálaigh C.J. also said that the only criterion or consideration for the court was whether the accused would abscond before trial or interfere with witnesses. The power to refuse bail on the basis that the accused might commit further offences was not included.

The following year, the Supreme Court revisited the issue of bail in *The People (Attorney General) v O'Callaghan* [1966] I.R. 501. In this case, a bail motion had been refused in the High Court, where Murnaghan J. set out, without reference to either *Purcell* or *Duffy*, a new and more extensive set of "matters which may be, and should be where appropriate, taken into account by the Court in considering whether or not it is likely that the prisoner may evade justice".

Murnaghan J. then stated that the following were issues to which the court was entitled to have regard:

(1) The nature of the accusation/the seriousness of the charge. The heavier the charge, the greater the chance that the accused would not appear to face it;

(2) The nature of the evidence in support of the charge. The more cogent the evidence, the greater the chance of conviction and consequently, the greater the likelihood that the prisoner would try to evade justice;

(3) The likely sentence on conviction—in this instance it was felt that the heavier the potential sentence, the more likely it would be that the prisoner would try to avoid it. The accused's previous record has a bearing on the probable sentence;

(4) The likelihood of more offences being committed while the accused was on bail. It was felt that a prisoner facing a long sentence would have nothing much to lose by committing further offences;

(5) The possibility of the disposal of illegally acquired property;

(6) The possibility of interference with witnesses and/or jurors;

(7) Failure to answer bail on a previous occasion;

(8) The fact that the prisoner was caught "red-handed";

(9) The objection of the Attorney General and/or the police authorities;

(10) The substance/reliability of the bailsmen offered; and

(11) The possibility of a speedy trial.

It was also suggested that bail might be refused in order to protect the prisoner.

On appeal to the Supreme Court, Walsh J. recognised that grounds 1, 2, 3, 5, 6, 7 and 8 were acceptable, but with certain reservations. The remaining grounds were deemed not to be so. In particular, ground number 4—the likelihood of the commission of further offences while on bail was held to be a matter which was in the view of the learned judge "quite unacceptable"—he stated that, "this is a form of preventative justice which has no place in our legal system and is quite alien to the true purpose of bail".

The Supreme Court held that certain factors would be relevant in ascertaining the likelihood that the accused person would attempt to evade justice. These are as follows:

(1) The seriousness of the charge;
(2) The nature of the evidence of the accused;
(3) The likely sentence upon conviction;
(4) The likelihood that unlawfully acquired property would be disposed of/destroyed;
(5) Interference with witnesses/jurors;
(6) Previous failure to answer to bail;
(7) Whether the accused had been caught red-handed;
(8) The objections of the Attorney General/Gardaí;
(9) The reliability/substance of the bailsmen; and
(10) The likelihood of a speedy trial.

It can be seen that most of these criteria can be categorised into two broad groups, namely, the evasion of justice and interference with the trial. The Supreme Court rejected the argument that the commission of further offences in the event of bail being granted was a valid ground upon which bail could be refused.

In an attempt to deal with the situation, s.11 of the Criminal Justice Act 1984 provides for the imposition of mandatory consecutive sentences in respect of offences committed while the accused person was on bail.

In *Ryan v Director of Public Prosecutions* [1989] I.R. 399, an argument that bail could be refused in order to prevent the commission of further offences was similarly rejected. Here it had been argued that the rights of those citizens who might become victims of crime should be taken into consideration when deciding whether or not to grant bail to an accused person. The argument was rejected because according to Finlay C.J., "the criminalising of mere intent has usually been the badge of an oppressive or unjust legal system".

This remained the position until the passing of the Sixteenth Amendment to Bunreacht na hÉireann following the bail referendum in 1996. Article 40.4.7 of Bunreacht na hÉireann now provides that, "provision may be made by law for the refusal of bail by a court to a person charged with a serious offence where it is reasonably considered necessary to prevent the commission of a serious offence by that person."

THE BAIL ACT 1997

The Bail Act 1997 (the "1997 Act") in s.1(2) defines "serious offence" as being any crime contained in the Schedule to the Act which attracts a possible custodial sentence of five years or more for an accused person of full capacity and with no previous convictions. The court is to have regard to factors outlined in s.2(2) when deciding whether bail ought to be denied. These are broadly similar to the list of grounds laid down in *O'Callaghan*, and in addition, the court may have regard to the fact that the accused person is addicted to a controlled substance. Effectively, therefore, the valid grounds upon which bail may be refused are those grounds which were upheld in *O'Callaghan* together with the new grounds set out in the 1997 Act.

REFUSAL OF BAIL

Section 2 of the 1997 Act provides that, "where an application for bail is made by a person charged with a serious offence", bail may be refused if the court is satisfied that such refusal is "reasonably considered necessary to prevent the commission of a serious offence". For bail to be refused under s.2 of the 1997 Act, the accused must be charged with a serious offence, as defined in s.1 and contained in the Schedule to the 1997 Act. Further offences have been appended to the Schedule by other pieces of legislation. In addition, the apprehended offence must also be a serious offence, although it is not required that the court be satisfied that the apprehended offence is a specific offence. Clearly though, s.2 cannot be invoked in the case of a person charged with serious offence where the apprehended offence is of a minor nature. The court must also be satisfied that the refusal of bail is "reasonably considered necessary". The 1997 Act requires that in determining the issue of bail the court *must* have regard to the following factors:

(i) the nature and gravity of the offence with which the accused is charged and the punishment likely to be imposed if he is convicted;

(ii) the nature and gravity of the apprehended offence and the likely punishment;

(iii) previous convictions (if any) of the accused;

(iv) previous convictions (if any) in respect of offences committed whilst on bail;

(v) the nature and strength of the evidence against the accused; and

(vi) any other offence with which the accused is charged and in respect of which he is awaiting trial.

BAIL

The court is entitled to have regard to any other factors in addition to those listed above. In *Maguire v Director of Public Prosecutions* [2004] 3 I.R. 241, the Supreme Court rejected the argument that a court, in deciding whether to grant bail, was confined to a consideration of the factors set out in s.2 of the 1997 Act to the exclusion of other factors relevant to the application.

If bail is refused under s.2(1) of the 1997 Act, provision is made in s.3 for the right of the accused to have the application for bail renewed if his trial has not commenced within four months.

Section 4 of the 1997 Act provides that where bail is being opposed under s.2, the accused's previous convictions cannot be referred to in a way that would prejudice the accused's right to a fair trial.

Section 5 of the 1997 Act relates to recognisances and provides that where bail is granted subject to recognisances, the accused person will not be released on bail until at least one-third of the amount of the recognisance be paid into court.

Section 6 provides for conditions which the court may impose on bail. Failure on the part of the accused to comply with these will lead to the rearrest of the accused and forfeiture of any recognisances.

SENTENCING

Prior to the passing of the Criminal Justice Act 1984 (the "1984 Act") , judges were entitled to exercise discretion with regard to imposing the appropriate penalties in respect of offences committed while the accused had been on bail.

Section 11 of the 1984 Act curbed this discretion somewhat by requiring the judge to impose a consecutive sentence for such offences. The section provided that:

> [A]ny sentence of imprisonment passed on a person for an offence committed after the commencement of this section while he was on bail shall be consecutive on any sentence passed on him for a previous offence, or if he is sentenced in respect of two or more previous offences, on the sentence last due to expire, so however that, where two or more consecutive sentences are required by this section are passed by the District Court, the aggregate term of imprisonment in respect of those consecutive sentences shall not exceed two years.

Section 11 of the 1984 Act was amended by s.10 of the 1997 Act. The effect of this amendment is that whereas s.11 of the 1984 Act required that mandatory consecutive sentences were imposed upon conviction for offences committed whilst on bail, s.10 of the 1997 Act additionally requires that a greater sentence be imposed in respect of such offences.

It might be argued, however, that both the sections are rendered toothless by their failure to prevent the judge from suspending the second (or even the first) of the sentences. The Irish judiciary have traditionally been quite hostile to any intrusion by the legislature into their discretionary powers with regard to sentencing.

In *The People v Noel Healy* [1989] 3 Frewen 188, the applicant was charged with a series of offences and was convicted and sentenced to concurrent terms of eight years on each count. He had been on bail when the offences were committed. When passing sentence, the judge took the total number of years which would be served into account and adjusted the sentence downwards. The applicant appealed against the severity of the sentence, arguing that he had received a much harsher punishment than his co-accused. During the appeal, counsel for the Director of Public Prosecutions submitted that the judge should disregard the duration of the sentence imposed for a previous offence and fix a sentence appropriate to the second crime—and not follow the English practice of taking account of the total number of years to be served. The Court of Criminal Appeal dismissed the application, holding that the sentence imposed on the accused was not excessive or founded on any error of principle, and that the comparison with the sentence handed down to the co-accused was inappropriate.

The question of suspending one of the consecutive sentences was raised in *The People (Director of Public Prosecutions) v Thomas Dennigan* [1980] 3 Frewen 253, in which case the applicant pleaded guilty to a series of offences contained in two bills of indictment—the second of which referred to offences allegedly committed whilst the accused was on bail in respect of the charges contained in the first bill.

With regard to the first set of charges, the accused was convicted and sentenced to concurrent sentences, the longest of which was a term of four years. He was then sentenced to five years for the second list of offences, to run concurrently with the first term. Counsel pleaded for leniency on his behalf due to personal circumstances, and said that the court could suspend one of the sentences on the basis that nothing in the 1984 Act prevented the judge from doing so. The court held that it could suspend a consecutive sentence, but that in this case, the offences committed were too serious. The court did, however, reduce each sentence due to the fact that not enough consideration had been given to the accused's personal circumstances.

Hearsay Evidence

Following the decision of the Supreme Court in *People (Attorney General) v McGinley* [1998] 2 I.L.R.M. 233 hearsay evidence may be adduced in support of an objection to bail under s.2 of the 1997 Act. The High Court had denied bail in that case on the basis of hearsay evidence from a member of the Gardaí. On appeal, the Supreme Court held that the accused retained the right to fair procedures which included the right to test the evidence against him through cross-examination *unless* special factors existed which could justify the use of hearsay evidence.

No provision is made in the 1997 Act or elsewhere for the compensation of an accused person who has been denied bail and who is subsequently acquitted. Finally, bail should not be set at such a high amount as to amount to a de facto refusal of bail.

Further Restrictions on Bail

Since the previous edition of this book, a number of legislative measures have been enacted which have a significant impact on the issue of bail.

(1) The Criminal Justice Act 2006 (the "2006 Act") created a number of specific offences relating to the *activities of criminal organisations*. The 2006 Act refers to "serious offences" *committed by, or in conjunction* with, criminal organisations and for the purposes of that 2006 Act, a "serious offence" is defined as one which attracts a sentence of four years or more. The 2006 Act also adds three "organised crime" offences to the list of offences contained in the Criminal Procedure Act 1967 with the effect that bail in respect of those *offences may only be granted on* application to the High Court. Of significance to this issue is the decision of the Supreme Court in *McDonagh v The Governor of Cloverhill Prison* [2005] IESC 4 where it was held *that bail could not be refused solely on the basis* that the applicant was involved in an ongoing feud.

(2) Part 2 of the Criminal Justice Act 2007 (the "2007 Act") amends the law on bail in a number of respects. Firstly, s.6 of the 2007 Act requires that an applicant for bail who is charged with a serious offence must furnish the prosecution with a statement containing details of any previous convictions and whether any of these convictions related to offences committed whilst on bail. The statement must also set out any previous applications for bail made by the applicant and the grounds upon which

such application(s) were based. Finally, the statement must contain specific information relating to the applicant's source of income including details of any property owned by the applicant which is valued in excess of €3,000.

Section 7 of the 2007 Act provides that where the State objects to the granting of bail, the opinion evidence of a Garda holding the rank of Chief Superintendent or higher, that bail should not be granted in order to prevent the commission of a further serious offence, may be admitted into evidence.

As previously stated, bail is a form of conditional release pending trial or appeal. The conditions to be attached to bail are determined by the court. Section 11 of the 2007 Act provides that among the conditions which may be imposed on the accused is that he wears an electronic monitoring device for the purpose of establishing his compliance, or non-compliance as the case may be, with the conditions of his bail. Section 11 has not yet been commenced. If/when it is commenced, it will apply to accused persons who are charged with a serious offence or those who are appealing against a custodial sentence imposed by the District Court.

Section 19(a) of the 2007 Act also provides that the Director of Public Prosecutions may appeal against the decision of the District Court to grant bail. The appeal lies to the High Court and was previously only available to an accused person who had been denied bail in the District Court.

KEY CASES AND LEGISLATION

The People (Attorney General) v O'Callaghan [1966] I.R. 501 and s.2 of the Bail Act 1997 (as amended)—Valid grounds for refusal of bail.

Maguire v Director of Public Prosecutions [2004] 3 I.R. 241—Court may have regard to any relevant factors in determining the issue of bail.

Types of Punishment

6

Upon conviction for a criminal offence, the court must then determine the nature and severity of the punishment to be imposed. In deciding, the court will have regard to certain factors, both aggravating and mitigating, and will adjust the sentence accordingly. Aggravating factors include the level of violence used, previous convictions and where there was a serious impact on the victim. Mitigating factors include co-operation with the Gardaí, the personal circumstances of the accused and whether the accused entered a plea of guilty, particularly at an early stage. The sentencing court must also have regard to the severity of the offence and to the personal circumstances of the offender.

IMPRISONMENT

Mandatory Sentences: A mandatory sentence is one which the court must impose. A conviction for murder will result in a mandatory life sentence regardless of any mitigating factors that may exist. The constitutionality of the mandatory life sentence for murder was upheld by the Supreme Court in *Lynch v Minister for Justice, Equality and Law Reform and Others* [2010] IESC 34 and *Whelan v Minister for Justice, Equality and Others* [2010] IESC 34. In the case of aggravated murder, s.3 of the Criminal Justice Act 1990 provides that a conviction for aggravated murder, which essentially replaces the offence of capital murder, attracts a mandatory life sentence with the stipulation that no fewer than 40 years be served.

Section 15 of the Misuse of Drugs Act 1977, as amended by the Criminal Justice Act 2007 provides for a mandatory *minimum* sentence of 10 years in respect of a conviction under that provision. Some discretion is allowed in this case; the mandatory minimum sentence need not be imposed where the judge is satisfied that there are sufficient reasons for not imposing it.

In most other cases, sentencing is a matter for discretion of the trial judge. Sentences for multiple offences can run concurrently. This means that where, for example, an accused is being sentenced for two offences, with 12 months' imprisonment being imposed for each offence, he will spend 12 months in prison, subject to whatever amount of remission he may be entitled to. If the sentences in the example just given were ordered to run consecutively, time will start to run in respect of the second sentence when the first sentence has been served. A judge can also direct that a sentence, or a part thereof can be suspended for a specified amount of time or. In the case of offences committed while on bail, sentences in respect of these *must* run consecutively as provided for by s.11 of the Criminal Justice Act 1984, as amended by s.10 of the Bail Act 1997.

FINES

A court may order that a convicted person may incur some financial penalty either in addition to, or instead of, a custodial sentence. The maximum amount to be imposed by the court will be laid down in the relevant Act. The maximum penalties that may be imposed in respect of summary offences and certain indictable offences are set down in the Fines Act 2009, which creates different categories of fines and the maximum amount which can be imposed in relation to each offence.

COMMUNITY SERVICE ORDERS

The Criminal Justice (Community Service) Act 1983 provides that any court other than the Special Criminal Court may order an offender to carry out unpaid community work. This form of punishment is imposed in lieu of a custodial sentence on offenders older than 16 years of age. The offender must consent to the making of the order, which will stipulate the number of hours to be worked. This number of hours cannot exceed 240.

FORFEITURE

The Proceeds of Crime Act 1996 makes provision for the forfeiture of property over a certain value, where the court is satisfied, on the civil standard of proof that such property was obtained as a result of criminal activity. The Act is enforced by the Criminal Assets Bureau set up by the Criminal Assets Bureau Act 1996. A conviction is not required prior to the confiscation of any property. In *Gilligan v Criminal Assets Bureau* [1998] 3 I.R. 185, the constitutionality of the Proceeds of Crime Act 1996 was upheld by the Supreme Court. It had been argued that the defendant's right to a trial in due course of law, as provided for by Art.38 of Bunreacht na hÉireann, had been infringed on the basis that the proceedings under the Act were of a criminal nature and that the application of the civil standard of proof was a clear violation of his Article 38 rights. This argument was rejected on the basis that the impugned provisions applied to property and not to individuals. The defendant had also argued that s.1(1) of the Act was unconstitutional on the basis that it operated retrospectively contrary to Art.15 of Bunreacht na hÉireann which prohibits the enactment of such legislation. The section provides that:

> [I]n this Act, save where the context otherwise requires—"proceeds of crime" means any property obtained or received at any time (whether before or after the passing of this Act) by or as a result of or in connection with the commission of an offence …

This argument was also rejected on the basis that, since the possession of unlawfully obtained property had not been lawful prior to the passing of the Act, it could not be argued that the Act had retrospectively criminalised conduct that had been lawful.

PROBATION

The issue of probation is governed by the Probation of Offenders Act 1907. Where a person has been convicted of an offence punishable by a custodial sentence, the provisions of the Act may be invoked. There are two ways in which this might happen:

(1) Where the offender has been tried in the District Court, s.1(1) of the Act may be applied. If the District Court judge is willing, no conviction is recorded against the offender although the court recognises that an offence has been committed.

(2) Where the offender has been convicted, the relevant court can order the release of the offender under s.1(2) of the Act. The offender must, however, enter into a recognisance to be of good behaviour for a period of up to three years. He will then be assigned a probation officer who will supervise him for the duration of his probation. Failure to abide by the terms of probation will result in the offender being sentenced for the original offence.

COMPENSATION

The Criminal Justice Act 1993 provides that courts have the power to order the payment of compensation to the victim of a crime, by the offender.

BINDING TO THE PEACE

An offender may be ordered to enter into a bond to keep the peace and be of good behaviour. This is effectively a form of conditional release whereby the offender signs an undertaking to abide by such conditions as are set down by the court for a specified period of time. In the event that these conditions are not observed, the court may order that the bond be forfeited or that the offender be committed to prison.

THE COURT POOR BOX

The court may dismiss the charge against the accused pursuant to the Probation of Offenders Act 1907, provided that the accused accepts responsibility for the offence and makes a donation to a charity.

CONSEQUENTIAL ORDERS

In addition to any sanctions which may be imposed upon conviction, there are a number of further orders which are a direct consequence thereof. These include:

(i) Notification requirements may be imposed on sex offenders pursuant to the Sex Offenders Act 2001 and on those convicted of drug trafficking offences pursuant to the Criminal Justice Act 2006.
(ii) Behaviour Orders, commonly referred to as "ASBOs" may be granted on application to the District Court pursuant to the Criminal Justice Act 2006.
(iii) Restriction on Movement Orders pursuant to the Criminal Justice Act 2006.

Elements of a Criminal Offence

7

The component parts of a criminal offence are the actus reus and the mens rea, both of which derive from the maxim *actus non facit reum nisi mens sit rea* (an act does not make a man guilty unless his mind be also guilty). If there is no actus reus there is no crime and where an act is carried out in the absence of any form of guilty intention there can be no conviction. The exception to this is where an offence is one of absolute liability, where mens rea is irrelevant, liability being imposed on proof that the prohibited conduct had been carried out. In the vast majority of cases, both elements of the offence must be established before criminal liability can be imposed.

THE BURDEN OF PROOF

The burden of proof in a criminal trial is placed on the prosecution. This refers to what the prosecution must do in order to prove its case against the accused, and was described in the following terms in *Woolmington v DPP* [1935] All E.R. Rep. 1: "throughout the web of the English criminal law one golden thread is always to be seen, that it is the duty of the prosecution to prove the prisoner's guilt …".

To discharge this burden, the prosecution must: (a) prove all the elements of the offence with which the accused is charged and; (b) disprove/negative any defences that are consistent with the innocence of the accused. This flows from the right of the accused to be presumed innocent until proven guilty. There are some exceptions to the general rule under the *Woolmington* principle where the burden of proof shifts to the accused: an example is where the defence of insanity is being put forward by the accused. In this instance, it will be for the accused to prove that he was insane at the time of the commission of the offence.

THE STANDARD OF PROOF

In criminal cases, the standard of proof is "beyond reasonable doubt". This means that even where the jury believes that it is possible that the accused committed the offence with which he is charged, they must acquit him if there is a reasonable doubt in their minds as to his guilt. In *The People (Attorney General) v Byrne* [1974] I.R. 1, the court stated that they must be satisfied beyond reasonable doubt that the accused committed the offence and also that the accused was entitled to the benefit of the doubt. Where, therefore, two interpretations of the accused's part in an alleged offence are possible, one being in his favour, the accused is entitled to be judged according to the more benign of the two, unless the jury is satisfied, beyond reasonable doubt, that the prosecution has established the contrary to the required standard. It should be remembered that "beyond reasonable doubt" does not necessarily mean "beyond all doubt". This point was clearly articulated by Denning J. in *Miller v Minister for Pensions* [1947] 2 All E.R. 372 where he stated that:

> "Proof beyond reasonable doubt does not mean proof beyond the shadow of doubt. The law would fail to protect the community if it admitted fanciful possibilities to deflect the course of justice. If the evidence is so strong against a man as to leave only a remote possibility in his favour which can be dismissed with the sentence 'of course it is possible but not in the least probable', the case is proved beyond reasonable doubt, but nothing short of that will suffice."

The standard of proof is lower in civil cases, where the plaintiff must prove his case on "the balance of probabilities". Where in a criminal case, the burden of proof shifts to the defence (e.g. the insanity defence), this burden is discharged on the civil standard which is the balance of probabilities.

THE ACTUS REUS

The actus reus is sometimes referred to as being the physical or action element of an offence. It should be remembered, however, that the actus reus can also include inaction or omission on the part of the accused.

Without the actus reus, there is no offence. It is impossible to sustain a prosecution for any offence on the basis of mens rea alone. In *R v Deller* (1952) 36 Cr. App. Rep. 184, the accused tried to sell a vehicle that he believed to be owned by a hire purchase company. He informed the purchaser that the car was legally his. Unknown to him, he was in fact the legal owner of the vehicle. He was acquitted of the offence of obtaining by false pretences because although he had the mens rea for the offence, there was no actus reus.

As stated previously, the actus reus need not necessarily be a positive act on the part of the accused, and can be established where there is a "state of affairs" or where the accused has omitted to act where he otherwise should have.

STATE OF AFFAIRS

In *R v Larsonneur* (1933) 29 Cox CC 673, the accused was convicted under the Aliens Order 1920 having been found in the UK. She had been sent out of the UK and had come to Ireland whereupon she was returned to the UK and handed over to the police. In *Winzar v Chief Constable of Kent* (1983) (*The Times*, March 28, 1983), the accused was convicted of being found drunk on the highway. He had been removed from a hospital by the police and had been put into a police car which had been parked on the highway. Despite the fact that in both these cases the offences could not be said to have been due to the voluntary actions of either accused, both resulted in convictions.

OMISSION

Criminal liability for omission arises where the accused is under some form of duty to act but fails to do so. In cases where there is no duty to act, no liability for failure to act will be incurred. A duty to act can arise in different circumstances:

(1) Statutory duty. Where a duty is imposed by a statute, failure to perform the obligations imposed amount to an offence.

(2) Contractual duty. Where, by virtue of a contract or by virtue of holding a particular office, duties are imposed on an individual, failure to carry out those duties may lead to a conviction. In *R v Dytham* [1979] 3 All E.R. 641, a police officer who failed to act to stop a brawl was convicted of misconduct. The court of Appeal in *Dytham* stated that the neglect of duty had to be wilful and not merely due to inadvertence. The court stated that the culpability of the accused must be "of such degree that the misconduct impugned is calculated to injure the public interest so as to call for condemnation and punishment". *Dytham* was cited with approval in Ireland in *DPP v Bartley*, unreported, High Court, June 13, 1997.

(3) Where the accused creates the danger, he may be convicted of an offence if he does nothing to mitigate its effects. In *R v Miller* [1983] 1 All E.R. 978, the accused was convicted of arson. He had accidentally started a fire and had done nothing to try to put it out. It was held that having started the fire, albeit by accident, he was then under a duty to extinguish it.

(4)   Voluntary assumption of duty: An accused can be convicted in circumstances where he has breached a duty owed to a third party in his care. In *R v Stone and Dobinson* [1977] 2 All E.R. 341, both defendants were convicted of manslaughter where they had failed to provide medical assistance for an elderly relative of the first-named defendant who had lived with them. In that case the duty had arisen in the case of the first-named defendant because he was related to the deceased. The duty imposed on the second-named defendant because she had assumed responsibility for the deceased. Further examples of instances in which criminal liability has been imposed on the basis of a voluntary assumption of duty are: *R v Bubb* [1851] 4 Cox CC 455; *R v Gibbins & Proctor* [1918] 13 Cr. App. Rep. 134 and *R v Taktak* [1988] 34 A. Crim. R. 334.

VOLUNTARINESS

The action(s) of the accused must be voluntary. Accordingly, where the accused has no control over his actions, there will generally be no conviction. This is discussed further in the chapter on Automatism.

THE MENS REA

This is the mental element of an offence. Where the accused has no mens rea, he cannot be convicted unless the offence is one of absolute liability. There are different degrees of mens rea which will be discussed separately.

INTENTION

In the context of criminal law, the term "intention" means the conscious objective or purpose of the accused. Intention is often confused with other concepts such as motive and the desire to achieve a particular result. It is important to note that intention is not the same as either one. One's motive for acting in a particular way is his reason for doing so. The presence of a motive may well be a factor from which guilt may be easier to establish but the absence of a motive does not mean that the accused has not committed the offence. The desire to bring about a particular result is not the same as intention either. An accused can be convicted even if the result of his action(s) is not what he desired. Where the intention of the accused forms a part of the offence, this must be proved beyond a reasonable doubt. Intention, as a form of mens rea, can be either *direct* or *oblique*.

Direct intention

This is where the accused wanted to bring about a particular result and carried out a deliberate act in order to achieve it.

Oblique intention

This form of intention is a more nebulous concept than direct intention and is premised on what the accused foresaw as being the result of his conduct. The actions of the accused are deliberate; but a result other than the one anticipated or desired comes about. The English courts have formulated and modified the test to be applied in cases of oblique intent and the following is a brief summary of those.

In *Hyam v DPP* [1974] 2 All E.R. 41, the defendant put burning newspaper through a letterbox causing the deaths of two children. Her *motive* was to frighten the owner of the house. She appealed her conviction for murder arguing that she had no intention to kill anyone. The House of Lords held that the conviction should stand if the prosecution could establish that when she had committed the act, she had known that it was *highly probable* that death or grievous bodily harm would result. In *R v Moloney* [1985] 1 All E.R. 1025, two men decided to compete with each other to see which of them was better at handling a shotgun. The defendant won and was then challenged by the deceased to fire the weapon. The accused duly fired and killed the deceased. In his defence, it was argued that because he was drunk, he had not considered the outcome of his actions. The House of Lords laid down a two-part test to be applied in cases such as this, and in doing so, departed from the "highly probable" test laid down in *Hyam*. The judge, in directing a jury should, where possible, avoid prescribing a definition of "intention" and leave it to the jury to decide. Where, however, an explanation should be given, the jury should be asked to consider two questions:

(1) Was the outcome a natural consequence of the voluntary act of the accused?
(2) Was this result foreseen by the accused as being a natural consequence of his actions?

If the answer to both was yes, then the jury would be entitled to infer that the accused intended to bring about the result.

In *R v Hancock and Shankland* [1986] 1 All E.R. 641, the two defendants were charged with murder, having thrown a concrete slab over a bridge resulting in the death of a driver in a car on the road below. The defence argued that they did not intend to kill the deceased and that they had acted as they did in a bid to prevent miners from breaking a picket. The trial judge directed the jury in accordance with the ruling in *Moloney*, that intent could be inferred if the defendants had foreseen that death or serious injury was a "natural consequence" of their actions. On appeal, the House of Lords rejected this and held that death or serious injury had to be a probable as well as a natural consequence. The jury, therefore, ought to have been told that intent could be inferred where death or serious injury was a "natural and probable" consequence and also that the higher the probability, the more likely it was that the accused had intended the result.

In *R v Nedrick* [1986] 3 All E.R. 1, the Court of Appeal modified the test again. The facts of this case were similar to those of *Hyam*, and the jury had been directed that the accused could be convicted if he was aware that it was "highly probable" that his actions would result in someone's death. The Court of Appeal held that the jury would be entitled to infer an intention to kill or seriously injure where the defendant recognised that death or serious injury as a result of his actions, was a "virtual certainty".

Finally, in *R v Woolin* [1999] 1 A.C. 82 the House of Lords held that where a result was virtually certain, it could be viewed as being the intended result. The leading Irish case is *The People (Director of Public Prosecutions) v Douglas and Hayes* [1985] I.L.R.M. 25. In that case, the defendants were appealing against their convictions for shooting with intent to kill, an offence contained in the Offences Against the Person Act 1861, on the basis that there had been no intention to kill. The Court of Criminal Appeal followed the decision of the House of Lords in *Hyam* and held that where there was evidence that a reasonable person would have foreseen that the natural and probable consequences of the defendants' conduct was that death would result, and that where it could be established that the defendants had acted recklessly, the jury was entitled to infer from that that the defendant had intended to cause death by his actions, subject to the requirement that both these facts be established beyond reasonable doubt.

THE PRESUMPTION OF INTENT

Section 4(2) of the Criminal Justice Act 1964 provides that, "the accused person shall be presumed to have intended the natural and probable consequences of his conduct, but this presumption may be rebutted". This section applies to the mens rea required for murder, but the presumption of intent applies to all offences in Irish law. In *The People (Director of Public Prosecutions v McBride* [1997] I.L.R.M. 233, the Court of Criminal Appeal held that the presumption of intent did not affect the presumption of innocence since it was "only a presumption and could be rebutted". In *The People (Director of Public Prosecutions) v Hull*, unreported, Court of Criminal Appeal, July 8, 1996, the court held that the presumption of intent should be regarded by the jury as being a two-step process, the first step being the determination of what the natural and probable consequences of the defendant's conduct were. If the jury accepted that the natural and probable consequence of the defendant's conduct was the death of the victim, the jury was entitled to conclude that the defendant had intended that consequence. The jury would then have to deal with the second step, which was to decide whether the presumption had been rebutted and that the direction of the trial judge to this effect had been correct.

RECKLESSNESS

This is a lesser form of mens rea than intention and arises where the accused has taken an unjustifiable risk. Recklessness can be objective or subjective. Subjective recklessness occurs where the accused was aware of the risk but decided to take it anyway. The leading English case on subjective reckless-ness is *R v Cunningham* [1957] 2 All E.R. 412, in which the court held that the test to be applied was whether the risk was in the mind of the accused. If the accused was aware of the risk and decided to take it, he was subjectively reckless in doing so. Objective recklessness occurs where the accused did not allude to the possibility that there was a risk which would have been obvious to the reasonable man. The test for objective recklessness was laid down in *Metropolitan Police Commissioner v Caldwell* [1981] 1 All E.R. 901, where the House of Lords held that the word "reckless" should be given its ordinary meaning and that where there was an "obvious risk", albeit one which was unknown to the accused, which the reasonably prudent person would have known about, the accused acted recklessly where he failed to appreciate it. The ruling in *Caldwell* was subsequently affirmed by the House of Lords in *R v Lawrence* [1981] 1 All E.R. 974. The main problem with objective recklessness, as defined in *Caldwell*, was that it did not cover situations in which the accused may have considered whether or not a risk existed but decided that there was none. Equally, the application of an objective test for recklessness under *Caldwell* meant that an accused was being judged against the standard of the reasonable man even where it was manifestly unjust to the accused to do so. It was also argued that having two different forms of recklessness, each judged according to different standards was in breach of art.6 of the European Convention on Human Rights which provides that anyone charged with a criminal offence is entitled to a "fair and public hearing within a reasonable time by an independent and impartial tribunal established by law". In *Elliott v C (A Minor)* [1983] 2 All E.R. 1005, the Court of Appeal upheld the conviction of a mildly mentally handicapped child who had set fire to a shed, on the basis that the risk attached to such conduct would have been obvious to the "reasonably prudent person". The effect of the so-called

"Caldwell loophole" was that no distinction was drawn between the accused who had knowingly taken a risk and the accused who had not considered whether there was a risk at all. The House of Lords finally overruled *Caldwell* in *R v G and R* [2003] 4 All E.R. 765, where it was held that a person acts recklessly when he takes an unreasonable risk in circumstances where the risk is known to him, knowing that a certain outcome is likely. The English courts have, therefore, reverted to a subjective test.

The position in Irish law, however, is not altogether clear. The decisions of the House of Lords are of persuasive authority only in this jurisdiction but it is arguable that the Irish judiciary are more flexible in their approach to various tests (see e.g. the rules on insanity).There also appears to be a greater preference for subjective tests in the Irish courts. The leading case in this jurisdiction on recklessness is *The People (Director of Public Prosecutions) v Murray* [1977] I.R. 360 where the two accused were charged with capital murder and argued that they did not have the necessary mens rea for that offence. The question for the court was whether Mrs Murray, who had fired the fatal shot, had acted recklessly by doing so. An essential component of the offence was knowledge or recklessness on the part of the accused as to whether the victim was a member of the Gardaí. In rejecting objective recklessness, the Supreme Court (per Walsh J.) stated that, "… in this context objective recklessness is really constructive knowledge; and constructive knowledge has no place in our criminal system in establishing intent".

The decision in *Murray* raises questions as to the application of subjective recklessness in cases other than capital murder. In that case, Henchy J. stated that the mens rea for capital murder is subjective without stating what the position was in relation to other offences. The same could be said of the judgments of Parke and Kenny JJ. The best that can be said is that although there appears to be a tendency towards the use of subjective tests, there are instances in which the court can apply an objective test. This can be seen in *Re Hefferon Kearns Ltd* [1993] 3 I.R. 191 and *PSS v JAS*, unreported, High Court, May 22, 1995.

CRIMINAL NEGLIGENCE

This form of mens rea applies to manslaughter only and is of a higher standard than the principles of negligence under the law of tort. In *The People (Attorney General) v Dunleavy* [1948] I.R. 95, it was held on appeal that to establish negligence sufficiently grave to sustain a conviction for manslaughter, the level of negligence would have to be considerably greater than would suffice in a civil action. Criminal negligence, being a more grave form of negligence, is judged objectively.

Negligence

Negligence, as a form of mens rea, really only arises where the offence in question requires that the accused failed to carry out some duty or acted in a way that breaches a duty. The duty in question is usually a statutory duty and negligence in this context is more akin to the concept of negligence in tort.

Strict liability/Absolute liability

These arise where certain conduct is prohibited and is then carried out by the accused. Only the actus reus need be established and the mens rea is not relevant. In some situations, an offence of strict liability may have a defence of reasonable belief/mistake.

COINCIDENCE OF ACTUS REUS AND MENS REA

In order to convict someone of a criminal offence, the prosecution must not only establish the elements of that offence (actus reus and mens rea) *and* disprove any/all defences raised on behalf of the accused, it must also show that:

(a) the actus reus and mens rea coincided, and
(b) the defendant's intentional and voluntary act *caused* the result. This does not arise in the case of a conduct offence.

(A) THE ACTUS REUS AND MENS REA MUST COINCIDE

Fundamentally, this means that the accused must have the mens rea to commit the offence in question when he is committing the actus reus element of the offence. Where the two do not coincide and cannot be shown to be a part of a continuing transaction, the accused will not be found guilty. A number of approaches have been formulated to deal with situations in which this problem arises.

(1) Continuing act

A number of acts, separate in themselves, can nonetheless be viewed as one continuing act. In *Fagan v Metropolitan Police Commissioner* [1968] 3 All E.R. 442, the accused accidentally parked his car on a policeman's foot. When asked to remove it, he refused. He argued that mens rea and actus reus did not coincide, and that consequently he could not be guilty of assault. The court held that the entire incident was a continuing act, the actus reus was already in place when the accused formed the mens rea for the offence by refusing to move the vehicle. A similar approach was adopted in *Kaitamaki v R* [1985] 2 All E.R. 435. In this case the court held that rape was a continuing act beginning with penetration and ending at withdrawal. The accused had realised after penetration that there was no consent on the part of the woman but carried on. At that point, he formed the mens rea for rape and as the actus reus was already in place, his conviction for rape was upheld.

(2) Duty

This approach was employed by the House of Lords in *R v Miller* [1983] 1 All E.R. 978. In this case, the accused had accidentally started a fire but did nothing to extinguish it. The Court of Appeal had upheld the conviction on the basis that it was a continuing act, having also looked at the duty approach. This approach imposes a duty on an individual to do something to mitigate the results of their conduct. Liability can then be imposed where the individual breaches that duty. The House of Lords stated that the duty approach was the better of the two in this case on the basis that a jury would find it easier to understand.

(3) The "supposed corpse rule"

The clearest example of this approach is to be seen in *Thabo Meli v R* [1954] 1 All E.R. 373. The accused, believing that he had killed someone whom he had assaulted, threw the "body" over a cliff. The victim died as a result of exposure rather than from the injury caused by the initial assault. In this case the conviction for murder was upheld on the basis that both acts were part of the one transaction. A similar decision was given in *R v Church* [1965] 2 All E.R. 72, where the Court of Appeal held that where different actions are part of the one plan a conviction could be sustained. Clearly, when the second act is an attempt to cover up the first act, a conviction is likely.

(B) CAUSATION

In result offences, a causal link must be established between the actions of the accused and the result of those actions. In *R v White* [1910] All E.R. 340 the accused had administered poison to his mother but the actual cause of her death had been heart failure. In this case the accused was convicted of attempted murder.

Whether or not a link exists between the actions of the accused and the outcome of those actions can be inferred from the surrounding circumstances. In *R v Cato* [1976] 1 All E.R. 260, the accused was convicted of manslaughter where his friend had died of an overdose of heroin. Both men were taking the drug and each man had handed the syringes to the other in order to inject the substance. Both men overdosed but the accused was saved. The Court of Appeal held that where the accused had injected the deceased and the deceased then died from the effects of the drug, a causal link had been established.

Novus Actus Interveniens

This concept arises in tort as well as in criminal law and in both situations may break the chain of causation with the result that the accused may be absolved of liability. It is essential that, in order for liability to be imposed, the causal link between the actions of the accused and the result of those actions is not broken. Where an act by either a third party or the defendant intervenes, the chain of causation may be broken. In the case of a novus actus by a third party, there is the requirement that the action is voluntary. In *R v Pagett* [1983] Crim. L.R. 394 the deceased had been placed against her will, by the defendant, in the firing line of bullets fired by the police who had been trying to arrest the accused. He appealed his conviction for murder arguing that the actions of the police amounted to a novus actus interveniens. This argument was rejected and the Court of Appeal also pointed out that the deceased had been placed in the situation, involuntarily, by the defendant. If the actions of the third party are calculated to protect him from the actions of the accused and where the actions by the third party are foreseeable by the accused, no novus actus interveniens will arise.

In addition, the actions of the third party must be unconnected to those of the accused and most amount to a new cause. In *R v Jordan* (1956) 40 Cr. App. Rep. 152, a conviction for murder was quashed. The accused had stabbed the victim causing him to be hospitalised. The victim's wound had actually almost healed but he died from pneumonia which was caused by a series of negligent acts carried out by doctors in the course of his treatment. The Court of Appeal held that the medical treatment had been "palpably wrong" and effectively held it to have been the cause of death. In *R v Smith* [1959] 2 All E.R. 193, the Court of Appeal held that where the original wound was an operating and substantial cause of death, the claim of causation would not be broken. In *R v Cheshire* [1991] 3 All E.R. 670, the Court of Appeal held that only treatment which could be described as extraordinary and unusual would amount to a novus actus interveniens and even then, it would have to be something that completely overshadowed the original wound.

THE EGGSHELL SKULL RULE

In tort, a plaintiff must take steps to mitigate his loss and his failure to do so will result in a smaller award of damages. This is not the case in criminal law. The accused is not entitled to expect his victim to take any steps which would lessen the effects of the accused's conduct. Equally, the accused must take his victim as he finds him and will not be able to rely on the fact that his victim suffered from some condition that renders him more susceptible to injury. In *R v Blaue* [1975] 3 All E.R. 446, the Court of Appeal refused to quash a conviction where the victim was a Jehovah's Witness and had refused a blood transfusion necessary following an attack on her by the accused. The defendant had argued that the victim would not have died had she accepted the blood transfusion. The Court of Appeal held that the victim's injuries had been caused by the defendant and that he could not then argue that her religious beliefs were unreasonably held in order to be absolved of liability.

KEY CASES AND LEGISLATION

Woolmington v DPP [1935] All E.R. 1—Prosecution bears the burden of proof.

Miller v Minister for Pensions [1947] 2 All E.R. 372—"Beyond reasonable doubt" does not mean "beyond all doubt".

The People (Attorney General) v Byrne [1974] I.R. 1—Accused entitled to acquittal where benign interpretation of the evidence is available.

R v Deller [1952] 36 Cr. App. Rep. 184—No offence where actus reus has not been committed.

R v Dytham [1979] 3 All E.R. 641—Criminal liability where contractual/ statutory duty not fulfilled.

R v Miller [1983] 1 All E.R. 978—Liability where accused failed to mitigate effects of his actions.

R v Stone and Dobinson [1977] 2 All E.R. 341—Liability imposed where accused breached voluntarily assumed duty.

Hyam v DPP [1974] 2 All E.R. 41; *R v Moloney* [1985] 1 All E.R. 1025; *R v Nedrick* [1986] 3 All E.R. 1; *R v Woolin* [1999] 1 A.C. 82; *The People (Director of Public Prosecutions) v Douglas and Hayes* [1985] I.L.R.M. 25—Oblique intention.

R v Cunningham [1957] 2 All E.R. 412—Subjective "Cunningham" recklessness.

Metropolitan Police Commissioner v Caldwell [1981] 1 All E.R. 901—Objective "Caldwell" recklessness.

R v G & R [2003] 4 All E.R. 765—Objective/Caldwell test for recklessness rejected. Subjective/Cunningham test affirmed by English courts.

Criminal Liability

Criminal Liability is imposed where the prosecution discharges the burden of proving that the accused committed the actus reus of the offence with which he is charged and that he did so having formed the necessary level of mens rea. If the prosecution goes on to disprove any defences put forward by the defence, the accused will be fixed with criminal liability in respect of the offence of which he has been convicted.

Secondary Participation

These are occasions where liability is imposed on individuals other than the person who actually committed the offence on the basis of what is called secondary participation. Secondary participation refers to any assistance given to the accused before, during or after the offence.

Traditionally, there were four categories of participation recognised by the common law and by the Accessories and Abettors Act 1861:

(1) Principal in the first degree—the person who actually committed the offence.

(2) Principal in the second degree—a person who aided or abetted the commission of an offence or who was present at the time of the commission.

(3) Accessory before the fact—a person who provided assistance prior to the commission of the defence.

(4) Accessory after the fact—a person who provided assistance to the person who committed a felony after the defence had been committed and "knowing that" a felony had been committed.

Section 8 of the Aiders and Abettors Act 1861 provided that any person who aided, abetted, counselled or procured the commission of a misdemeanour was liable to be prosecuted as a principal offender.

The Criminal Law Act 1997 repealed the older legislation and the relevant provisions are contained in ss.7 and 8 of the 1997 Act.

Section 7(1) provides that, "any person who aids, abets, counsels or procures the commission of an indictable offence shall be liable to be indicted, tried and punished as a principal offender".

In the case of summary offences, a similar provision to that contained in s.7(1) of the Criminal Law Act 1997 is to be found in s.22 of the Petty Sessions (Ireland) Act 1851.

In order to be "indicted, tried and punished" as a principal offender, an offence must actually be committed. This is also the case in respect of persons charged with summary offences. This differs from the situation in which a person is charged with an inchoate offence. An inchoate offence (attempt, conspiracy or incitement) is an offence in itself.

Both Acts refer to a person who "aids, abets, counsels or procures".

(1) AIDING

To aid someone in the commission of an offence is to knowingly provide assistance in its commission. It is not required that the person providing such assistance is present at the scene of the crime.

In *Gillick v West Norfolk and Wisbech Area Health Authority* [1985] 3 All E.R. 402, it had been argued that a doctor who prescribed contraceptives for an underage girl would be aiding and abetting in the commission of an offence. The House of Lords held that this might be the case depending on the intention of the doctor and was not dependant upon the doctor's presence at the time/location of the actual offence. Similarly, in *The People (Director of Public Prosecutions) v O'Reilly* [1991] 1 I.R. 77 it was held that the provision of a vehicle for the purpose of a burglary could lead to a conviction for aiding that offence even though the accused had not actually taken part in the burglary itself.

(2) ABETTING

This term is more often than not used in conjunction with the term "aiding" and for all intents and purposes, appears to mean the same thing.

(3) COUNSELLING

This term refers to encouragement or advice given prior to the commission of the offence. The encouragement need not have been the cause of the offence. In *R v Calhaem* [1985] 2 All E.R. 266, the defendant told a man to kill a woman whom the accused regarded as being a "love-rival". The accused appealed against her conviction and argued that there had been no causal link between what she had said and the death of the victim. The Court of Appeal held that no causal link was required; where there had been some form of contact between the accused and the killer this would suffice. In *R v Gianetto* [1996] Crim. L.R. 722 the trial judge stated that:

"Supposing somebody came up to (the defendant) and said 'I am going to kill your wife', if he played any part, either in encouragement, as little as patting him on the back, nodding, saying 'oh goody', that would be sufficient to involve him in the murder, to make him guilty, because he is encouraging the murder."

(4) PROCURING

This occurs where the desired outcome is achieved through some effort on the part of the accused. In *Attorney General's Reference (No. 1 of 1975)* [1975] 2 All E.R. 684 it was held that there did not have to be any agreement between the parties nor any encouragement on the part of the accused.

"You procure a thing by setting out to see that it happens and taking the appropriate steps to produce that happening." (per Widgery L.J.)

ACTUS REUS OF SECONDARY PARTICIPATION

There must be some evidence that actual assistance was provided to the principal offender. The level of assistance need not be very high as can be seen from *Gianetto*, but there will be no secondary liability imposed where a person merely happens to be at the scene of a crime or fails to stop the commission of a crime. The exception to this general rule is where there is a duty to intervene and that duty is not fulfilled, as occurred in *Dytham*. Another exception exists where the perpetrators of the offence derive some encouragement from the presence at the scene of the crime of the accused. In *R v Clarkson* [1971] 3 All E.R. 344, it was held that for liability to be imposed in such a situation, the fact that the perpetrators of the offence were encouraged by the presence of the accused was not enough in itself. The court held that the prosecution would have to prove that the accused had intended to encourage the commission of the offence. In *The People (Attorney General) v Ryan* [1966] 1 Frewen 304, the Court of Criminal Appeal adopted the same position and in *The People (Director of Public Prosecutions) v Rose*, unreported, Court of Criminal Appeal, February 21, 2002, a murder conviction was overturned on the basis that words uttered by the appellant could not be shown to have encouraged in the commission of the offence.

MENS REA OF SECONDARY PARTICIPATION

It must be shown that the accessory to the offence intended to assist the principal offender and that the accessory knew that an offence was being committed by the principal offender. Intention in this context relates to encouragement or assistance in the commission of the offence. Knowledge that an offence is to be committed appears to be enough. In *The People (Director of Public Prosecutions) v Madden* [1977] I.R. 336, a conviction was upheld where the accused provided a vehicle knowing that the vehicle was to be used in a violent crime. Similarly, in *The People (Director of Public Prosecutions) v Egan* [1989] I.R. 681, a conviction for robbery was upheld even though the accused did not know that an armed robbery had been planned. Liability was imposed on the basis that he had provided the robbers with a place to store a vehicle that had been used in the commission of the offence knowing that a "small stroke" was to take place.

A victim of an offence will not be convicted as an accessory despite the fact that they could be said to "facilitate" or encourage its commission. An example would be where a man is charged with incest under the Punishment of Incest Act 1908 (as amended by the Criminal Law (Incest Proceedings) Act 1995). The female in that situation will not be deemed to be an accomplice, particularly in view of the fact that the Act seeks to protect people from being victims of the offence.

Section 7(2) of the 1997 Act provides that where a person, knowing that an arrestable offence has been committed, acts with the intention of preventing the arrest of a guilty party he is guilty of an offence.

THE DOCTRINE OF COMMON DESIGN (JOINT ENTERPRISE)

Although there are similarities between the doctrine of common design and secondary participation, the main difference is that under the doctrine of common design, where two or more agree to commit an offence, each party is a principal offender whereas secondary participants are complicit in offences carried out by principals. In the former, all parties *are* principal offenders whereas in the latter the parties are dealt with *as though they were* principal offenders.

This, however, would appear to be becoming more of an academic or theoretical distinction rather than a practical one. Dicta from various judgments of the Court of Criminal Appeal suggest that the judiciary regard the two concepts as being interchangeable. In *R v Anderson and Morris* [1996] 2 All E.R. 644 the Court of Appeal held that:

> "[W]here two persons embark on a joint enterprise, each is liable for the acts done in pursuance of that joint enterprise, that includes unusual

consequences if they arise from the execution of the agreed joint enterprise but ... if one of the adventurers goes beyond what has been tacitly agreed as part of the common enterprise, his co-adventurer is not liable for the consequences of that unauthorised act."

The main point to be taken from that definition is that where there is an agreement to carry out an offence, all parties to that agreement are liable. But where one party goes further than what was agreed and does something else that was not foreseeable to the other parties, then they are not liable for this unsanctioned activity.

The issue of foresight was also discussed in *Chang Wing-Siu v R* [1985] A.C. 168 where the three accused, armed with knives, set about committing a robbery, during which a person was stabbed and later died as a result. The accused were each charged with murder and their defence was that although they had brought knives along in order to carry out the robbery, there had been no intention to use them. Their argument was that the knives had been used in self-defence and that neither accused had foreseen the actual use of the knives. The trial judge directed the jury that if the defendants had foreseen serious bodily harm or death as a possibility, this would be enough to convict them even where they did not intend the eventual outcome. On appeal, it was held that the trial judge's direction had been correct and that where the prosecution could show that the use of the weapon was foreseen by the defendants as being a real possibility, this would suffice for a conviction for murder arising from a joint enterprise. This is so even where it would have to be established that the actual killer must have had the required mens rea for murder. In *The People (DPP) v Murray* [1977] I.R. 360, the defendants, a married couple, were involved in a bank robbery. They were pursued by Gardaí and Mrs Murray shot and killed a garda. Both were convicted of capital murder. On appeal the Supreme Court held that there had been a common design in relation to the robbery and to the use of violence and also with regard to murder, but that there was no common design with regard to capital murder because there was no evidence to suggest that there had been an agreement on the use of violence against the Gardaí.

However, in both *The People (Director of Public Prosecutions) v Pringle* [1981] 2 Frewen 57 and *The People (Director of Public Prosecutions) v Eccles*, unreported, Court of Criminal Appeal, February 10, 1986, the Court of Criminal Appeal found that there had been a common design in respect of capital murder. The difference between these cases and the *Murray* case is that in *Pringle* and *Eccles*, there had been some evidence of the intention to overcome the Gardaí using whatever force was necessary whereas no such evidence existed in *Murray*.

In *The People (Director of Public Prosecutions) v Doolan* [2002] 4 I.R. 463, the accused had hired another man to carry out a punishment beating but told him not to shoot the victim. The victim died from shotgun wounds to the leg. The defence argued that the joint enterprise went no further than the punishment beating and that the use of the shotgun had been outside the scope of the original agreement. The court applied *R v Anderson and Morris* and concluded that there had been a common design and that it had been agreed that the victim would suffer serious injury. That being enough to prove murder, the use of the gun, even though it had not been sanctioned, was not outside the scope of common design.

Withdrawal from complicity

If an accessory calls off the arrangement before the crime is committed they will not be liable for any offences carried out after they have withdrawn. It was held that the withdrawal should be communicated to the other participants, and in *R v Jensen and Ward* [1980] V.R. 1904 it was held that withdrawal should either be communicated or that some positive step should be taken such as calling the police.

Vicarious Liability

At common law, no one can be held liable for the crimes of another. This was pointed out in *Hardcastle v Bielty* [1982] 1 Q.B. 709. There are some instances arising mainly out of an employer/employee relationship where an employer may be liable for the criminal acts of his employee, where the employee is acting within the scope of his employment. The issue can also arise under the Intoxicating Liquor Acts.

Strict Liability

These offences are mostly statutory offences. Where a strict liability offence is created by statute, the wording used will indicate the level of mens rea required. Until recently, s.1 of the Criminal Law Amendment Act 1935 provided for the offence of statutory rape. This offence required proof of mens rea for the first two parts of the actus reus, i.e. (i) sexual intercourse, (ii) with a female, (iii) who is under the age of 17, the third part of the actus reus did not require any mens rea, the man's knowledge or belief regarding the female's age being irrelevant.

Absolute Liability

These offences require no mens rea whatsoever and are complete when the actus reus is committed.

Criminal Liability of Corporations

At common law, a corporation could not be held criminally liable, notwithstanding the fact that they are viewed as persons by the law. Practical considerations also applied—not all penal sanctions could be imposed on a corporation.

However, it is possible to impose criminal liability on a corporate entity in some situations. To determine corporate liability for criminal acts the question to be answered was whether the act was carried out by someone who had control within the company, such as would enable him to direct the activities of the company. In *Tesco Supermarkets v Nattrass* [1972] A.C. 153, the House of Lords held that a regional manager employed by the plaintiff company could not be regarded as senior enough within the company to enable him to direct the mind and will of the company. A corporation cannot be held liable for the fraudulent acts of employees where the fraud is perpetrated against the company itself. This was held in *Canadian Dredge and Dock Co. v R* [1985] I.S.C.R. 662. It need hardly be said that there are certain crimes which are incapable of being committed by a company, e.g. bigamy, but there are a number of so-called "corporate crimes" which are governed by legislation. Section 8 of the Environmental Protection Agency Act 1992 and s.11 of the Air Pollution Act 1997 are two examples of statutory provisions that impose criminal liability on companies for offences under those Acts. In *Alphacell Ltd v Woodward* [1972] A.C. 824, the House of Lords had to decide whether, for the purposes of the offence in question which involved pollution of a river, the defendant had to have intended to cause the pollution. It was held that this was not necessary; liability for the pollution could be established by showing that the pollution was caused by the defendant. The word "cause" was to be given its ordinary meaning and the House of Lords essentially held that, but for the activities of the defendant, the pollution would not have occurred. This was enough to impose liability for the offence in question. Similar reasoning was used by the Supreme Court in *Maguire v Shannon Regional Fisheries Board* [1994] 2 I.L.R.M. 253. However, in *Shannon Regional Fisheries Ltd v Cavan County Council* [1996] 3 I.R. 267, Keane J. in a dissenting judgment, stated that there were some offences which necessitated the establishment of mens rea. Where the only punishment for an offence is a custodial sentence, a company cannot be convicted of it.

TRANSFERRED INTENT

There are situations where liability may be imposed even where the actual victim of the defendant's action is not his intended target. In these situations, the defendant's malice towards his intended victim is deemed to have been transferred to his actual victim. In *R v Latimer* (1886) 16 Cox C.C. 70 the defendant had intended to hit one person but missed, hitting and injuring another person instead. He appealed his conviction on the basis that he had not meant to injure the actual victim. His conviction was upheld on the grounds that his malicious intent had been transferred from his intended target to the injured party.

The doctrine of transferred intent is also provided for in some statutory provisions, an example being s.4(1) of the Criminal Justice Act 1964 which provides that, "where a person kills another unlawfully the killing shall not be murder unless the accused intended to kill, or cause serious injury to, *some person, whether the person actually killed or not*" (emphasis added). Similar provisions are to be found in s.6 of the Non-Fatal Offences Against the Person Act 1997 in relation to syringe offences.

The doctrine does not apply in situations where there is no similarity between the mens rea for the intended offence and that which is required for actual offence with which the defendant is charged.

LIABILITY OF CHILDREN FOR CRIMINAL OFFENCES

At the time of writing the previous edition of this book, the defence of Infancy provided an absolute defence to children younger than seven years of age against criminal prosecution. The defence was based on the common law doctrine of *doli incapax* which regarded children under a certain age as being incapable of forming mens rea. The phrase *doli incapax* simply means "incapable of crime". In this jurisdiction, children were categorised into different age groups for the purposes of criminal liability.

The enactment of the Children Act 2001 heralded a major departure from the existing statutory framework for dealing with children who committed criminal offences. The provisions of the 2001 Act which would have raised the age of criminal responsibility from seven years of age to 12 years were never enacted and those sections have since been amended by the Criminal Justice Act 2006 which repeals the defence in respect of children aged between 7 and 14 years of age and provides a general commitment not to prosecute children under the age of 12 years of age for most criminal offences. For this reason, this section is now included in the chapter on liability for criminal offences rather than the section on defences. For comparative purposes, the rules pertaining to the criminal liability of children prior to the commencement of Pt V of the Children Act 2001 (as amended) are set out below.

CHILDREN UNDER THE AGE OF SEVEN YEARS

A child under the age of seven years was conclusively presumed to be *doli incapax*. This presumption could not be rebutted, regardless of the actual understanding of the child or the circumstances in which the alleged offence takes place. The effect of the presumption was to prohibit the prosecution of children under the age of seven years in any circumstances.

CHILDREN BETWEEN 7 AND 14 YEARS

Children between 7 and 14 years of age were presumed to be *doli incapax*. The difference between this group and those in the younger age group was that if the child was older than 7 and younger than 14 years of age, the presumption of *doli incapax* could be rebutted where there was evidence of a "mischievous discretion". The standard required to rebut the presumption was quite high and required that the child knew that his conduct went beyond mere mischief. The test was whether the child appreciated the seriousness of his actions. In *R v Gorrie* (1919) 83 J.P. 136, the court held that the child had to know that his conduct was gravely or very seriously wrong. This test was followed in this jurisdiction in *KM v Director of Public Prosecutions* [1994] 1 I.R. 514.

Until the passing of the Criminal Law (Rape)(Amendment) Act 1990 a boy younger than 14 years of age was conclusively presumed to be incapable of committing rape. This presumption applied to the offence of rape only and did not preclude the prosecution of a boy under the age of 14 for other forms of sexual assault. This presumption was abolished by s.6 of the Criminal Law (Rape)(Amendment) Act 1990 with the result that, provided the presumption of *doli incapax* was rebutted, a boy aged between 7 and 14 years of age could be charged with rape.

THE CHILDREN ACT 2001

Prior to the amendments effected by the Criminal Justice Act 2006, Pt V of the Children Act 2001 sought to raise the age of criminal responsibility to 12 and stated that, "it shall be conclusively presumed that no child under the age of 12 years is capable of committing an offence". Section 52(2) provided that, "there is a rebuttable presumption that a child who is not less than 12 but under 14 years of age is incapable of committing an offence because the child did not have the capacity to know that the act or omission was wrong". These provisions would have had the effect of widening the group of children who were conclusively presumed to be *doli incapax* and narrowing the group of children to whom a rebuttable presumption applied. The section was never commenced and has since been amended significantly by s.129 of the Criminal Justice Act 2006.

THE CRIMINAL JUSTICE ACT 2006

The current position regarding the liability of children for criminal offences is set out in s.52 of the Children Act 2001, as substituted by s.129 of the Criminal Justice Act 2006. The substituted section provides that:

(i)   Children under the age of 12 shall not be charged with a criminal offence. This is a general commitment not to prosecute children and is subject to the exception that a child aged 10 or 11 may be charged with murder, manslaughter, rape, aggravated sexual assault or rape under s.4 of the Criminal Law (Rape)(Amendment) Act 1990. The reference to the capacity of the child to commit an offence has been removed.

(ii) The common law doctrine of *doli incapax* insofar as it pertained to children between the ages of 7 and 14, is abolished.

(iii) A child under the age of 14 years of age may only be prosecuted by or with the consent of the Director of Public Prosecutions.

In addition, s.53 of the Children Act 2001 (as amended) provides that where a member of An Garda Síochána believes on reasonable grounds that a child who is younger than 12 years of age has committed an offence other than murder, manslaughter, rape, aggravated sexual assault or rape contrary to s.4 of the Criminal Law (Rape)(Amendment) Act 1990, the member must endeavour to bring the child to his/her parent(s) or guardian(s).

KEY CASES AND LEGISLATION

Section 52 of the Children Act 2001 as substituted by s.129 of the Criminal Justice Act 2006—Criminal liability of children.

Homicide

9

The term "homicide" denotes the unlawful killing of a human being. The circumstances of any particular case, coupled with the level of mens rea on the part of the accused, will determine whether the homicide is murder, manslaughter or infanticide. Suicide is no longer a criminal offence in this jurisdiction, having been abolished by s.2(1) of the Criminal Law (Suicide) Act 1993. Aiding and abetting the suicide of another person remains an offence under s.2(2) of that Act.

MURDER

Murder has always been an offence at common law. The most frequently quoted common law definition of murder is that of Coke C.J.:

> "Murder is when a man of sound memory, and at the age of discretion, unlawfully killeth within any country of the realm any reasonable creature in rerum natura under the King's peace with malice afore-thought either expressed by the party or implied by law, so as the party wounded, or hurt, etc. die of the wound, or hurt, etc. within a year and a day of the same."

The common law definition still holds true but with a number of modifications. Firstly, the mens rea for murder is now contained in s.4 of the Criminal Justice Act 1964 which provides in s.4(1) that:

> Where a person kills another unlawfully the killing shall not be murder unless the accused intended to kill, or cause serious injury to, some person, whether the person actually killed or not.

Section 4(2) provides that, "[t]he accused person shall be presumed to have intended the natural and probable consequences of his conduct, but this presumption may be rebutted".

Secondly, it is no longer the case that the death has to occur within a year and a day of the injury. The so-called "year and a day rule" was abolished by s.38 of the Criminal Justice Act 1999.

Thirdly, the common law definition requires that the accused be "of sound memory, and of the age of discretion". This simply means that the accused must be sane and over the age of criminal responsibility. Since the passing of the Criminal Justice Act 2006, the age of criminal responsibility is 10 years of age, where the accused is charged with murder, manslaughter, rape, rape under s.4 of the Criminal Law (Rape) (Amendment) Act 1990 or aggravated sexual assault. A child who is under the age of 14 years may only be prosecuted with the consent of the Director of Public Prosecutions, in accordance with the provisions of the 2006 Act.

Finally, the requirement at common law that the victim be "any reasonable creature *in rerum natura*" means that the victim must have been a human being, born alive. It is arguable, given the acknowledgement of the right to life contained in Art.40.3.3 of Bunreacht na hÉireann, that this common law rule has been extended to include the unborn. Termination of pregnancy is an offence under the Offences Against the Person Act 1861 which carries a maximum sentence of life imprisonment. It is permissible in this jurisdiction only if there is a risk to the life of the mother, in accordance with the judgment of the Supreme Court in *Attorney General v X* [1992] 1 I.R. 1.

CAUSATION

Murder is a result offence and therefore, it must be shown that the accused caused the unlawful death. Where the link between the accused's conduct and the victim's death is broken by a novus actus interveniens, the accused will not be liable.

ATTEMPTED MURDER

In order to prove the charge of attempted murder, the prosecution must show that the accused carried out the actus reus with the *intention to kill*. The accused cannot be convicted of attempted murder if the mens rea was the intention to cause serious injury.

PENALTY ON CONVICTION

Murder is an indictable offence and carries a mandatory sentence of life imprisonment.

AGGRAVATED MURDER

The offence of aggravated murder is contained in s.3 of the Criminal Justice Act 1990 (the "1990 Act"). The aggravating factor is the identity of the victim or where the killing is carried out in the course of the commission of certain offences under the Offences Against the State Act 1939. The unlawful killing of any of the following people will amount to aggravated murder:

(1) A member of An Garda Síochána acting in the course of his duty;
(2) A prison officer acting in the course of his duty; or
(3) The Head of a foreign State, a member of the government of a foreign state or a foreign diplomat, where the murder is committed within this State in furtherance of a political objective.

Section 3 of the 1990 Act also applies to attempts to carry out any such murders.

This offence replaces the offence of capital murder which was an offence punishable by death. The death penalty was abolished by s.1 of the Criminal Justice Act 1990 and s.4 of that Act provides that the penalty for aggravated murder is a mandatory life sentence with the specification that a minimum term of 40 years be served.

MANSLAUGHTER

Manslaughter is a common law offence and arises in two ways, voluntary and involuntary.

VOLUNTARY MANSLAUGHTER

Where the accused has committed the actus reus for murder and has the mens rea for that offence but successfully pleads either provocation or excessive self-defence, he will be acquitted of murder but convicted of manslaughter. This is because these two defences are partial defences which reduce the offence from murder to manslaughter. An acquittal will never be justified since, by definition, the accused has committed the actus reus of murder with the necessary mens rea. The justification for the reduction of the offence to manslaughter is that the mens rea was caused by the action(s) of the deceased. From the point of view of the accused, the main benefit of this reduction is that the mandatory life sentence is avoided, leaving the penalty, which can be anything up to life imprisonment, to be decided by the judge.

INVOLUNTARY MANSLAUGHTER

Involuntary manslaughter occurs where the accused does not have the mens rea for murder, but where the victim dies as a result of the actions or sometimes the omissions of the accused. There is, therefore, no mens rea for manslaughter per se; the offence occurs where, but for the availability of either provocation or excessive self-defence (voluntary manslaughter), the accused would be convicted of murder or, alternatively, where the actions of the accused lead to the unintended death of the victim (involuntary manslaughter). Liability for involuntary manslaughter can arise in any one of three different ways.

(1) A criminal and dangerous act

The leading case on this type of manslaughter in this jurisdiction is *The People (Attorney General) v Crosbie and Meehan* [1966] I.R. 490 where the Court of Criminal Appeal held that in order to sustain a conviction for manslaughter, the act causing the death of the victim had to be unlawful and dangerous. The issue of whether an act is dangerous is for the jury to decide. In *The People (Director of Public Prosecutions) v Hendley,* unreported, Court of Criminal Appeal, June 11, 1993, the Court of Criminal Appeal held that in addition to the requirement that the act causing death be unlawful and dangerous, it was also necessary to show that it had been deliberate.

(2) Criminal negligence

This occurs where an otherwise lawful act is performed with such a high level of negligence that any reasonable person would have been aware that it carried a substantial risk of serious injury. In *R v Adomako* [1994] 3 All E.R. 79, the House of Lords held that in order to decide whether the accused had been criminally negligent, the jury had to ask the following questions:

(i) Was there negligence as that term is understood in the context of civil law?
(ii) Was the victim's death caused by the negligence of the accused?
(iii) In acting as he did, had the accused deviated considerably from the standard of care which would have been expected of him?

Where these questions were answered in the affirmative, the accused could be convicted of manslaughter.

In *The People (Attorney General) v Dunleavy* [1948] I.R. 95, the Court of Criminal Appeal held that the jury should be told that a very high degree of negligence had to be established in the case of manslaughter. The test is objective and the accused's subjective belief in the reasonableness of his actions is irrelevant. Similarly, in *The People (Director of Public Prosecutions) v Cullagh,* unreported, Court of Criminal Appeal, March 15, 1999 it was stated that the negligence of the accused had to be shown to be "gross negligence" and that the ordinary standard of negligence in civil cases could not be enough to sustain a conviction for manslaughter.

(3) Breach of duty

Where the accused refuses or neglects to fulfil a duty that is imposed on him by virtue of a contract, a statute, his relationship with the victim, his office or by his own assumption of a duty to care for the victim, a conviction for manslaughter may result where the victim dies as a result of that breach of duty by the accused. In *R v Instan* [1893] 17 Cox C.C. 602, the accused refused to provide food or medical assistance for an elderly relative with whom she lived. This refusal led to the death of the victim and the accused was convicted of manslaughter. Similarly, in *R v Stone and Dobinson* [1977] 2 All E.R. 341, convictions for manslaughter were returned where the two accused had failed to provide medical help for a dependant relative who lived with them. The court held that in the case of the first defendant, the duty had arisen from his blood relationship to the deceased and in the case of the second defendant the duty had arisen because she taken it upon herself to carry out certain tasks for the deceased. Once this responsibility had been accepted, a duty had been assumed by the second defendant and that breach of duty resulted in a conviction for manslaughter. Further examples of convictions arising from breach of duty can be seen in *R v Senior* (1899) 19 Cox C.C. 219 and *R v Taktak* (1988) 34 A. Crim. R. 334.

PENALTY ON CONVICTION

The penalty is at the discretion of the court.

INFANTICIDE

The offence of infanticide is a very narrowly defined one and is provided for by the Infanticide Act 1949. Section 1 of the Act creates the offence which is the killing of an infant (under one year of age), through an act or omission that would otherwise be murder, by the mother of the infant who, at the time of the offence was suffering from the effects of pregnancy, childbirth and/or lactation, with the result that her mind was adversely affected. The offence is based on the recognition that a woman may well be suffering from physical and emotional/psychological ill-effects of pregnancy and childbirth, but is illogical in the sense that the offence only applies to the killing of a child under the age of one year.

PENALTY ON CONVICTION

Section 6(3) of the Criminal Law (Insanity) Act 2006 provides that "a woman found guilty of infanticide may be dealt with in accordance with subs.(1)". Section 6 of the 2006 Act provides for diminished responsibility. The 2006 Act is dealt with in the chapter on Insanity. Prior to the passing of the 2006 Act, the penalty for a woman convicted of infanticide was left to the discretion of the court and was dealt with as manslaughter.

EUTHANASIA

Section 2(2) of the Criminal Law (Suicide) Act 1993 renders it an offence to aid, abet, counsel or procure a suicide or an attempted suicide by another person. This is the case even though neither suicide nor attempted suicide is an offence. Nonetheless, any person who intentionally kills another is guilty of murder and his motivation for doing so, however, well-intentioned is irrelevant as is the "consent" of the victim. It is not unlawful to withdraw or withhold medical treatment, even where to do so will result in death. Where a patient refuses medical treatment or requests that it be discontinued and the patient is of sufficient capacity to make that decision, such a request must be acceded to. In *Re a Ward of Court (Withdrawal of Medical Treatment)* [1996] 2 I.R. 79, the Supreme Court held that the so-called "right to die" is regarded as being a corollary of the constitutionally protected right to life and an expression of the unenumerated rights of bodily integrity which was held in *Ryan v Attorney General* [1965] I.R. 294 and privacy, held in *McGee v Attorney General* [1974] I.R. 284 and *Kennedy v Ireland* [1987] I.R. 587.

Sexual Offences

10

The law pertaining to sexual offences has traditionally condemned three types of sexual conduct: sexual activity carried out in the absence of the consent of one of the parties, sexual conduct carried out where one of the parties lacks capacity to give legal consent and that which, although engaged in consensually, was deemed to be inherently wrong on the basis that it was repugnant to traditional moral standards.

Rape is the clearest example of the first of these categories, but despite the moral and legal condemnation it attracted, a man could not be convicted for raping his wife until the "marital rape exemption" was abolished by the Criminal Law (Rape) (Amendment) Act 1990. Additionally, the law did not recognise male rape until the passing of the Act.

The law in relation to the second type of sexual conduct has also undergone a radical change following the Supreme Court decision in *CC v Ireland & Ors* [2006] IESC 33 which struck down s.1(1) of the Criminal Law Amendment Act 1935 as unconstitutional on the basis that a man charged with unlawful carnal knowledge of a girl under the age of 15 years did not have a defence of reasonable mistake available to him. In *A v The Governor of Arbour Hill Prison* [2006] IESC 45, the applicant, who had been charged, tried and convicted of the offence which had been struck down by the Supreme Court in *CC v Ireland*, challenged the legality of his continued detention in respect of the offence. His application was granted by the High Court and he was duly released from custody. This decision was subsequently overruled by the Supreme Court and the applicant was then rearrested. The Criminal Law (Sexual Offences) Act 2006 was rushed through the Oireachtas in the wake of the case of "Mr A" and the offences contained within it are applicable to both sexes.

Finally, the law has traditionally also criminalised activity which, even when carried out by consenting adults, was deemed sufficiently harmful to the moral fabric of society to warrant criminal sanction. The most obvious example of this category of offence was the offence of buggery which had been covered by ss.61 and 62 of the Offences Against the Person Act 1861. This offence was abolished by s.3 of the Criminal Law (Sexual Offences) Act 1993.

This chapter looks at the main offences of a sexual nature covered by Irish law.

Rape

Section 2(1) of the Criminal Law (Rape) Act 1981 (the "1981 Act") provides the statutory basis for what is still referred to as "common law rape". Rape is committed where a man has sexual intercourse with a woman, who at the time of the intercourse does not consent and where the man either knows that the woman does not consent or is reckless as to whether or not she consents.

The actus reus of rape is having sexual intercourse with a woman who does not consent. The mens rea is knowledge of, or recklessness as to, the absence of the woman's consent.

Rape under the 1981 Act is a gender specific offence which can only be carried out by a man against a woman. Until the passing of the Criminal Law (Rape) (Amendment) Act 1990 (the "1990 Act"), a man could not be convicted of raping his wife due to the requirement at common law that in order to convict for rape, sexual intercourse had to be "unlawful", and since this meant outside marriage, husbands were granted a "marital rape exemption". Section 5 of the Criminal Law (Rape) (Amendment) Act 1990 abolished this requirement although the consent of the Director of Public Prosecutions is still required before a prosecution for rape within marriage can be brought. Another exemption existed in respect of boys under the age of 14 who were con-clusively presumed to be incapable of rape. This presumption was abolished by s.6 of the 1990 Act and consequently, a boy under the age of 14 (but older than 7) could be prosecuted, provided that the presumption of *doli incapax* has been rebutted. This position has changed as a result of the passing of the Criminal Justice Act 2006 and currently, a boy of 10 may be charged with rape, provided that the consent of the Director of Public Prosecutions is granted.

For the purposes of s.2(1) of the 1981 Act, sexual intercourse means vaginal intercourse only. The offence is complete upon penetration, which must be proven. In *The People (Attorney General) v Dermody* [1956] I.R. 307, it was held that the slightest penetration would suffice.

Consent

Absence of the woman's consent is part of the actus reus and this must be established. Consent must be freely given and where consent is subsequently withdrawn, the man must desist or he may be liable to a charge of rape. The same applies where the man realises that there is no consent on the part of the woman. In *Kaitamaki v R* [1984] 2 All E.R. 435, it was held that rape was a continuing act and that the accused was guilty of the offence when he continued having intercourse after he had become aware that the woman did not consent.

Vitiating factors

Consent may be vitiated where it is induced by fraud. In *R v Flattery* (1877) 13 Cox C.C. 388 and *R v Williams* [1922] All E.R. 433, convictions for rape were returned where the consent of the complainants had been induced by fraudulent misrepresentations as to the nature of the act. The complainant in the first case had been told that she was having a surgical procedure carried out and the complainant in the second case had been told that she was undergoing a procedure that would improve her singing voice. The fraudulent misrepresentation must be in relation to the nature of the act of sexual intercourse. In *R v Linekar* [1995] 3 All E.R. 69 the accused was acquitted of raping a prostitute. She had agreed to have intercourse with him in return for a specified sum of money which was then not paid. There was evidence that indicated that the accused had no intention of paying. This, however, did not amount to fraud for the purpose of gaining consent to sexual intercourse. The complainant had agreed to have intercourse with the accused and the fact that he made off without paying her did not have any relevance to the issue of consent.

The woman must be capable of giving consent. In *R v Mayers* (1872) 12 Cox C.C. 311 and in *The People (Director of Public Prosecutions) v X*, Central Criminal Court, *Irish Times*, May 20, 1995 it was held that a sleeping woman was incapable of giving consent. Similarly, consent may be vitiated where it is induced by intoxication. In *R v Camplin* [1845] 1 Cox C.C. 220, the accused was convicted of rape where he had caused the complainant to become intoxicated and then had sexual intercourse with her. In *R v Lang* [1975] 62 Cr. App. Rep. 50, the Court of Appeal held that it is the effect of the intoxicant on the complainant and not the fact that she consumed it that is relevant and that where a woman is incapable of exercising judgement due to intoxication, consent will not be valid.

Submission and failure to resist

Failure to resist is not the same as consent. Section 9 of the Criminal Law (Rape) (Amendment) Act 1990 provides that failure to offer resistance does not of itself constitute consent. The jury is entitled to take this matter into account and may infer consent where no evidence of resistance is adduced.

Submission to sexual intercourse is not the same as consenting to it. Where the complainant submits to intercourse due to fear or intimidation, consent is not freely given. In *R v Olugboja* [1981] 3 All E.R. 443, it had been argued by the defence that the complainant had been "persuaded" to have sexual intercourse with the accused. The Court of Appeal held that a jury in a rape trial should be told that consent and submission are not the same and that while consent involves submission, the reverse is not always true.

MENS REA

As previously stated, the mens rea for rape, as with most sexual offences, is the man's knowledge of the woman's lack of consent or his recklessness to that fact. In the situation where a man believes that the woman is consenting, the question arises as to whether an honest belief is enough or whether it must also be reasonable. Section 2(2) of the 1981 Act states that where this issue is raised, the jury is to have regard to the presence or absence of reasonable grounds for the defendant's belief. The test has both subjective and objective elements; the defendant's honest belief is relevant but the jury must then determine whether the defendant had any reasonable grounds upon which to base his belief. This approach was eventually adopted in England following the decision of the House of Lords in *DPP v Morgan* [1975] 2 All E.R. 347. In that case, the House of Lords held that an honest belief, however unreasonably held, meant that an accused could not be convicted of rape. In this jurisdiction the jury in a rape trial need only be directed as to the provisions of s.2(2) if the accused claims that he believed that the woman was consenting. This is clear from the wording of the provision itself and was held to be the case by the Supreme Court in *The People (Director of Public Prosecutions) v McDonagh* [1996] 1 I.R. 565.

RECKLESSNESS

The test for recklessness is likely to be subjective. In *The People (Director of Public Prosecutions) v Creighton* [1994] 1 I.L.R.M. 551, the Court of Criminal Appeal stated that recklessness was the same as heedless conduct. The test in English law is subjective. In *R v Satnam and Kewel* [1988] Crim. L.R. 236, the Court of Appeal held that where the defendant had continued having intercourse regardless of the woman's consent, the jury was entitled to conclude that he had acted recklessly.

PENALTY ON CONVICTION

Rape is an indictable offence and is punishable by a maximum sentence of life imprisonment.

RAPE UNDER S.4 OF THE CRIMINAL LAW (RAPE) (AMENDMENT) ACT 1990

This section deals with offences of a penetrative nature other those covered by s.2 of the Criminal Law (Rape) Act 1981. Unlike rape under the 1981 Act, the offences covered by s.4 of the 1990 Act are drafted in gender-neutral terms. There are two elements to the actus reus:

(a) Penetration of the anus or mouth by the penis, or
(b) Penetration of the vagina by any object held or manipulated by another person.

Clearly, the offence contained in the first category may only be committed by a male and it may be committed against a male or a female. The offence in the second category may be committed by a male or a female but only against a female.

The mens rea is not stated in the section itself, but given that an offence under s.4 is one of sexual assault, albeit one which involves penetration, it makes sense to regard the mens rea for sexual assault as being applicable, with the same being the case in relation to the issue of consent.

PENALTY ON CONVICTION

Rape under s.4 is an indictable offence and is punishable by a maximum sentence of life imprisonment.

SEXUAL ASSAULT

Section 2 of the 1990 Act gives statutory expression to the common law offences of indecent assault upon a male person and indecent assault upon a female person. Both offences are now combined in a gender-neutral form in the section. The actus reus of sexual assault is the same as that for the offence of assault under s.2 of the Non-Fatal Offences Against the Person Act 1997 with the additional requirement that it be carried out in circumstances of indecency. This means that two things must be established, namely, assault and circumstances of indecency.

Assault occurs where the accused either intentionally or recklessly, directly or indirectly, applies force to the body of the complainant or where the accused causes the complainant to reasonably fear that he will be subjected to immediate physical contact to which he does not consent. Consent, therefore, is a defence to a charge of sexual assault, provided, of course, that consent is freely given by a person with the capacity to give it.

The second element of the actus reus is that the assault must take place in circumstances which are indecent. What amounts to indecency will depend on the facts of each case but where there is uncertainty, the guidelines laid down by the House of Lords in *R v Court* [1988] 2 All E.R. 221 may be of some assistance. In that case, the House of Lords categorised different types of conduct under three headings:

(i) Acts which are not inherently indecent. An example might be where the accused removes someone's coat. This is not an inherently indecent act and the fact that the accused derives some form of gratification from doing it will not suffice to render it an indecent act.

(ii) Acts which are inherently indecent, regardless of the motive of the accused. These will suffice for the purpose of establishing circumstances of indecency.

(iii) Acts which may be indecent depending on the circumstances. In determining whether these acts are indecent, the jury should have regard to how they might be viewed by right-minded people, taking the relationship between the parties and the reason for the accused's actions into consideration.

PENALTY ON CONVICTION

Sexual assault under s.2 of the 1990 Act is an indictable offence carrying a maximum term of five years' imprisonment.

AGGRAVATED SEXUAL ASSAULT

Section 3 of the 1990 Act deals with the offence of aggravated assault. Essentially, this is a more serious form of the offence under s.2 of the Act and comprises sexual assault coupled with the use or threat of serious violence, grave humiliation, degradation or injury.

The actus reus has two elements; the intentional assault in circumstances of indecency and the use or threat of serious violence, grave humiliation, degradation or injury. There are two parts to the mens rea also; the intention to commit an indecent assault and the intention to use or threaten to use serious violence, grave humiliation, degradation or injury.

Consent may not be a defence to an offence under s.3 of the 1990 Act. The section envisages activity of a much graver nature than that which is contemplated by s.2. An analogy might be drawn with s.4 of the Non-Fatal Offences against the Person Act 1997 which creates the offence of "causing serious harm". Consent is not a defence to that offence and it seems reasonable to suppose that given the nature of the offence under s.3 of the 1990 Act, as reflected by the potential penalty attracted by it, that consent would not be a defence to a charge of aggravated sexual assault either.

In *R v Brown* [1993] 2 All E.R. 75, the House of Lords refused to allow a defence of consent to charges of assault causing actual bodily harm. The case involved a group of sadomasochists who had inflicted injuries, some of which required hospitalisation, on each other. The defendants argued that they had participated in the conduct consensually and that their convictions should be overturned. When the House of Lords ruled against them, they brought a case before the European Court of Human Rights, arguing that their rights under the European Convention on Human Rights had been breached. In *Laskey, Saggard and Brown v UK* [1997] 24 E.H.R.R. 39, the European Court of Human Rights held against the applicants, stating that the defendant had the right and the duty to protect vulnerable sectors within society and that this did not breach any right asserted by the applicants under the Convention.

PENALTY ON CONVICTION

Aggravated sexual assault is an indictable offence and carries a maximum sentence of life imprisonment.

STATUTORY RAPE

A girl who is under the age of consent (17 years) cannot, by definition give consent to sexual intercourse. Therefore, regardless of the girl's willingness to engage in sexual intercourse, no defence of consent can avail an accused.

The legislation governing this issue was until recently the Criminal Law Amendment Act 1935, s.1(1) of which provided that the unlawful carnal knowledge of a girl who is under the age of 15 was an offence regardless of any purported consent on the part of the girl and regardless of the belief on the part of the man that the girl was older than 15. Section 2 of the 1935 Act provided that the unlawful carnal knowledge of a girl between the ages of 15 and 17 was also an offence, albeit a less serious one.

Consent on the part of the girl was irrelevant as was the belief on the part of the man that the girl was older than 17. In effect, these offences, commonly referred to as "statutory rape", were offences of absolute liability; all that had to be established was the age of the girl and that sexual intercourse had taken place. Section 1(1) of the 1935 Act was struck down by the Supreme Court as being repugnant to the terms of Bunreacht na hÉireann in *CC v Ireland & Ors* [2006] IESC 33 on the basis that an accused did not have any defence of honest mistake available to him.

HONEST MISTAKE

In response to the Supreme Court's ruling the Oireachtas passed the Criminal Law (Sexual Offences) Act 2006. Section 2 of the Act replaces s.1(1) of the 1935 Act with a similar provision but provides in s.2(3) that:

it shall be a defence to proceedings for an offence under this section for the defendant to prove that he or she honestly believed that, at the time of the alleged commission of the offence, the child against whom the offence was alleged to have been committed had attained the age of 15 years.

Where the accused relies on the defence of honest mistake, the Act provides that the court shall have regard to the presence or absence of reasonable grounds for such belief. Although the only provision struck down as being repugnant to the terms of Bunreacht na hÉireann was s.1(1) of the 1935 Act, s.1(2) which provided that the attempted defilement of a girl under the age of 15, and s.2 which provided for similar offences in respect of girls between 15 and 17 were repealed by s.3 of the Criminal Law (Sexual Offences) Act 2006. The new offences are drafted in gender-neutral terms and consequently, apply to offences against males as well as females. The defence of honest mistake is similarly available to these offences.

DEFILEMENT OF A CHILD UNDER THE AGE OF 15 YEARS

Section 2 of the Act provides that it is an offence for any person to engage in a sexual act with a child who is younger than 15 years of age or to attempt to do so. The Act defines "sexual act" as an act consisting of sexual intercourse or buggery between persons who are not married to each other or an act described in s.3(1) or 4(1) of the Criminal Law (Rape) (Amendment) Act 1990. Where the accused raises the defence of honest mistake as to the age of the child, the court must consider whether there were reasonable grounds for the belief of the accused. Consent by the child is not a defence. The offence under s.2 carries a maximum penalty of life imprisonment.

DEFILEMENT OF A CHILD UNDER THE AGE OF 17 YEARS

The offence created by s.3 of the Act is committed in the same way as the offence under s.2. The difference between the two offences is the age of the child against whom the offence is committed. The penalty for this offence is a maximum term of 5 years' imprisonment or, if the accused is a person in a position of authority in relation to the child, to a term of up to 10 years' imprisonment. In the case of an inchoate offence under s.3, the penalty is a maximum term of imprisonment of 5 years and in the case of a person in a position of authority, a maximum of 10 years' imprisonment, in accordance with s.5 of the Criminal Law (Sexual Offences)(Amendment) Act 2007. The section provides that in the case of subsequent commission of the offence, longer terms of imprisonment may be imposed. The defence of honest belief is available to the accused and if raised, the court will have regard to the presence or absence of reasonable grounds for the belief.

An offence under s.2 or s.3 may be tried summarily if:

(i) the court is of the opinion that the facts alleged constitute a minor offence capable of being tried summarily;

(ii) the accused, having been informed of his right to trial by jury, does not object to the summary disposal of the case; and

(iii) the Director of Public Prosecutions consents to the summary trial of the offence.

If tried summarily, the Act provides for the imposition of lesser penalties. Somewhat curiously, the Act provides that a female child under the age of 17 will not be found guilty of an offence under the Act by reason only of having engaged in sexual intercourse. This provides a positive defence to females which is denied to males and accordingly, has been identified by many commentators as being discriminatory having regard to the equality provisions of Bunreacht na hÉireann.

REPEAL OF CERTAIN OFFENCES BY THE CRIMINAL LAW (SEXUAL OFFENCES) ACT 2006

Following the decision of the European Court of Human Rights in *Norris v Ireland* [1991] 13 E.H.R.R. 186 the Oireachtas passed the Criminal Law (Sexual Offences) Act 1993. Under the provisions of the 1993 Act, the offence of buggery as contained in s.61 of the Offences Against the Person Act 1861 was abolished, thereby decriminalising this form of sexual activity between consenting male adults. Section 3 of the 1993 Act contained offences of buggery against males under the age of 15 and between 15 and 17 respectively. This section has now been repealed by ss.2 and 3 of the Criminal Law (Sexual Offences) Act 2006.

Section 11 of the Criminal Law (Amendment) Act 1885 provided that it was an offence to commit or attempt to commit any act of gross indecency, whether in public or in private. The Act provided no definition for "gross indecency", but essentially the offence amounted to sexual activity between males excluding buggery. Section 11 of the 1885 Act had been repealed by s.4 of the Criminal Justice (Sexual Offences) Act 1993 which provided that it was an offence to commit or attempt to commit acts of gross indecency with males under 15 years of age or with males between 15 and 17. This, too, has been repealed by s.2 and 3 of the 2006 Act.

Sexual Offences against Mentally Ill Persons

Section 5 of the Criminal Law (Sexual Offences) Act 1993 creates the offences of:

(1) intercourse with a mentally impaired person or an attempt to have intercourse with a mentally impaired person;
(2) buggery or attempted buggery of a mentally impaired person;
(3) acts or attempted acts of gross indecency by a male against a male who is mentally impaired.

Mental impairment is defined in s.5 as "suffering from a disorder of the mind, whether through mental handicap or mental illness which is of such a nature or degree as to render a person incapable of living an independent life or of guarding against serious exploitation".

Defences

(1) Marriage—where the accused is married to the mentally impaired person or has reasonable grounds to so believe, no offence is committed.
(2) Lack of knowledge—where the accused did not know and had no reason to suspect that the person was mentally impaired, the accused will have a defence on this basis.

The jury must have regard to the accused's state of mental health also and where the accused is of limited intelligence, this factor should be borne in the minds of the jury.

Incest

The Punishment of Incest Act 1908, as amended by the Criminal Law (Incest Proceedings) Act 1995, makes it an offence to engage in sexual intercourse with someone who is closely related by blood. Consent is not a defence.

Incest by a Male

Incest by a male is committed where a man has sexual intercourse with a woman who is to his knowledge his mother, sister, half-sister, daughter or granddaughter. The offence is not committed if there is no blood relationship between the accused and the woman.

INCEST BY A FEMALE

Incest by a female is committed where a woman over the age of 17 permits her father, grandfather, brother, half-brother or son to have sexual intercourse with her, knowing that they are related by blood.

For the purposes of the offence of incest, sexual intercourse is vaginal intercourse only.

SEXUAL EXPLOITATION

The provisions of the Criminal Law (Sexual Offences) Acts 1993 and 2006 are aimed at protecting individuals who may be vulnerable, by reason of age or mental infirmity, to sexual predators. In addition, the Sexual Offences (Jurisdiction) Act 1996 confers jurisdiction on the Irish courts to try people who are alleged to have committed sexual offences against children younger than 17 years of age in a foreign country. In order to permit the trial of such individuals, the Act requires that the offence with which the accused is charged in the foreign jurisdiction is an offence recognised by Irish law.

The Child Trafficking and Pornography Act 1998 was enacted with the objective of combating international paedophile rings who rely on the availability of children. The Act has been amended by the Criminal Law (Sexual Offences) Amendment Act 2007 and more recently by the Criminal Law (Human Trafficking) Act 2008. The Act seeks to achieve this objective by setting out a number of offences. Section 3 of the Act provides that it is an offence to organise or knowingly facilitate the entry into or exit from the State of a child for the purpose of the sexual exploitation of the child. It is also an offence to provide accommodation for a child for the purpose of sexual exploitation. This offence is clearly directed at those who are involved in paedophile rings and is committed regardless of whether the accused physically abuses the child or not. The offence carries a maximum penalty of life imprisonment. Where a person takes, detains or restricts the liberty of a child for the purpose of sexual exploitation or uses the child for this purpose, he will be liable on conviction to a term of imprisonment of for life. Sexual exploitation is broadly defined in the Act and includes the use of the child for prostitution or pornographic purposes.

The making or possession of child pornography is also an offence under the Act. The Criminal Law (Human Trafficking) Act 2008 is concerned with the trafficking of adults and children for the purpose of exploitation. Exploitation is defined in the 2008 Act as labour exploitation, sexual exploitation or exploitation consisting of the removal of one or more organs of the person.

THE SEX OFFENDERS ACT 2001

The Sex Offenders Act 2001 contains a number of provisions which impose certain obligations on individuals convicted of any of the sexual offences to which the 2001 Act applies. The relevant offences are contained in the Schedule to the Act and where further offences have been created since the passing of the 2001 Act, these may also be subject to the requirements of the Act. The obligations imposed by the Act exist alongside any penal sanction imposed by the court in respect of such offences and the Act provides for the length of time for which these obligations are effective. Part 2 of the Act imposes obligations on sex offenders to provide the Gardaí with certain information concerning their name, home address or any other address used by them. This is commonly referred to as the "sex offenders register" although no such register exists. Sex offenders convicted in another jurisdiction are also amenable to the provisions of the Act. Part 3 of the Act provides for Sex Offenders Orders which are granted on the application of a member of the Gardaí not below the rank of Chief Superintendent where the court is satisfied that the order should be granted in order to protect the public. The order prohibits the person named within it from carrying out certain types of conduct specified in the order.

KEY CASES AND LEGISLATION

The People (Attorney General) v Dermody [1956] I.R. 307—Offence complete upon penetration, however slight.

Kaitamaki v R [1984] 2 All E.R. 435—Rape is a continuing act.

R v Flattery (1877) 13 Cox C.C. 388 and *R v Williams* [1922] All E.R. 433—Consent vitiated by fraud.

R v Olugboja [1981] 3 All E.R. 443—Consent must be freely given and submission does not equate with consent.

CC v Ireland & Ors [2006] IESC 33—Failure to provide for defence of honest mistake in cases of "statutory rape" in the Criminal Law Amendment Act 1935 held to be unconstitutional. Defence now contained in s.2 of the Criminal Law (Sexual Offences) Act 2006.

Non-Fatal Offences Against the Person

11

Prior to the enactment of the Non-Fatal Offences Against the Person Act 1997, the law in relation to non-fatal offences was contained primarily in the Offences Against the Person Act 1861 (the "1861 Act"). The 1861 Act contained many specifically defined offences and was often criticised for being overly technical. The Non-Fatal Offences Against the Person Act 1997 modernised the law in relation to these types of offences and also created certain new offences.

ASSAULT

The offence of assault is contained in s.2(1) of the 1997 Act. Section 2(1) provides that an assault is committed where the defendant, without lawful excuse and without consent, intentionally or recklessly;

(a) directly or indirectly applies force to or causes an impact upon the body of another or
(b) causes another to believe on reasonable grounds that he or she is likely to be immediately subjected to the direct or indirect application of such force or impact.

Section 2 therefore encompasses the common law offences of assault which is now contained in s.2(1)(b) and battery which is provided for by s.2(1)(a).

The actus reus is the direct or indirect application of force, or causing an impact to the body of another, or causing the other person to believe on objectively reasonable grounds that the application of such force or the causing of such impact is imminent. The absence of the victim's consent is also a part of the actus reus. The mens rea is intention or subjective recklessness.

Consent

Consent may be either express or implied. No offence under s.2 will be committed where:

(i) the defendant did not know or believe that his conduct was unacceptable to the other person; or
(ii) the force was not intended to injure and was unlikely to do so; or
(iii) the conduct is no more that what is to be expected as part of everyday life.

Words as a form of assault

Section 2 of the Act is silent on the issue of whether mere words can amount to an assault. Clearly, words would not suffice for s.2(1)(a). At common law, words were not capable of constituting an offence unless they were accompanied by some threatening gesture. In *Tuberville v Savage* (1669) 1 Mod. Rep. 3, words were held to negative an assault where the accused had put his hand on his sword and told the victim that, "if it were not assize time, I would not take such language". In effect, the accused had told the victim that he was not going to assault him. The common law rule appears to have been abolished by s.2 which provides that an assault is committed where the accused "causes another to believe on reasonable grounds" that the application of force is imminent.

Force

Section 2(2) of the Act defines "force" and provides that force includes the application of heat, light, electric current, noise or any other form of energy or the application of matter in any form.

Immediacy

The victim must believe that the direct or indirect application of force will be immediately forthcoming.

Punishment on conviction

Assault under s.2 of the 1997 Act is a summary offence only and is punishable by a maximum sentence of six months' imprisonment and/or a fine.

ASSAULT CAUSING HARM

Section 3 of the 1997 Act provides that, "a person who assaults another, causing him or her harm shall be guilty of an offence". Harm is defined in s.1 of the Act as being "harm to the body or mind and includes pain and unconsciousness".

The actus reus of an offence under s.3 has two components, both of which must be established. It must be shown that the accused has committed an assault as defined in s.2 and that harm, as defined in s.1 has resulted. In *R v Ireland* [1997] 4 All E.R. 225, the House of Lords held that an assault causing actual bodily harm had been committed by the accused where a number of his victims had suffered psychological trauma as a result of receiving silent telephone calls from the accused.

The mens rea of an offence under s.3 of the 1997 Act is intention or subjective recklessness. Section 3 does not explicitly state this, but given that an offence under s.3 is essentially the same as an offence under s.2 with the added requirement that harm be shown, the mens rea of a section 3 offence can be implied from the wording of s.2.

PUNISHMENT ON CONVICTION

An offence under s.3 may be tried summarily or on indictment. On summary conviction the penalty is a maximum term of imprisonment of 12 months and/or a fine. On conviction on indictment, the penalty is a maximum term of imprisonment of five years and/or an unlimited fine.

CAUSING SERIOUS HARM

Section 4 of the 1997 Act provides that, "a person who intentionally or recklessly causes serious harm to another shall be guilty of an offence". "Serious harm" is defined in s.1 as being "an injury which creates a substantial risk of death or which causes serious disfigurement or substantial impairment of the mobility of the body as a whole or of the function of any particular bodily member or organ".

The actus reus of this offence is causing serious harm. It is not necessary to prove the elements of an assault for the purposes of s.4. In many cases, the level and nature of the injury sustained will imply an assault but it is important to note that assault is not a part of the actus reus of an offence under s.4.

The mens rea is intention or subjective recklessness. The accused must have mens rea with regard to the dangerous conduct and to the likelihood that serious harm would be caused by it.

Consent

Absence of consent is an integral part of the actus reus of an offence under s.2, and by implication under s.3. Since it is not necessary to show that an assault has taken place to establish the actus reus of an offence under s.4, the question arises as to whether consent may be a defence to such an offence.

It would appear that consent is not generally a defence to serious harm but there may be exceptional circumstances in which it might amount to a defence. The issue arises in the context of sport and in this regard, the Court of Appeal has held that only conduct which is "sufficiently grave to be properly characterised as criminal" should lead to a prosecution. In *R v Barnes* [2005] 1 W.L.R. 910, the accused was charged with unlawfully and maliciously inflicting grievous bodily harm contrary to the Offences Against the Person Act 1861. The incident occurred in the course of a football match where the accused was said to have injured the victim with a "crushing, late, unnecessary, reckless and high" tackle from behind. In addition to stating the required gravity of the conduct, the Court of Appeal said that unless the conduct complained of went beyond what a player could reasonably be regarded as having accepted by participating in the sport, he will be regarded as having implicitly consented to the injury.

The case of *R v Brown* [1993] 2 All E.R. 75 has already been discussed in the context of sexual offences, but is also relevant to a discussion of consent in the context of serious harm.

The difference between the judgment of the respective courts in *Brown* and *Barnes* does not readily permit of a logical explanation. Both involved the voluntary participation of consenting adults. In *Attorney General's Reference (No. 6 of 1980)* [1981] 2 All E.R. 1057, the House of Lords accepted that consent provided a defence in certain circumstances such as properly conducted games and sports and stated that, "[t]hese apparent exceptions can be justified as ... needed in the public interest".

The House of Lords also stated that, "... it is not in the public interest that people should try to cause or should cause each other actual bodily harm for no good reason".

It seems, therefore, that where the conduct in question is deemed to be beneficial to the public interest, consent will provide a defence. The social benefit derived from sporting activities appears to be what differentiates it from the type of conduct engaged in *Brown*. The case law thus suggests that public policy considerations will take precedence over the individual's consent even in the context of conduct carried out privately.

PUNISHMENT ON CONVICTION

An offence under s.4 is tried on indictment and carries a maximum penalty of life imprisonment and/or an unlimited fine.

THREATS TO KILL OR CAUSE SERIOUS HARM

Section 5 of the Act provides that:

> a person who, without lawful excuse, makes to another a threat, by any means intending the other to believe it will be carried out, to kill or cause serious harm to that other or a third person shall be guilty of an offence.

The actus reus of this offence is making a threat to kill or cause serious harm. The method of making such a threat is irrelevant. The mens rea is the intention to make the threat coupled with the intention that the victim believes that the threat will be carried out.

There are both similarities and differences between this offence and that of assault. If a threat is made that is capable of being immediately carried out, an offence under both sections has been committed provided that the threat is to kill or cause serious injury. One difference between the two offences is that whereas an assault centres around the immediacy of the threat, an offence under s.5 does not. Another difference is that for an assault to take place, the victim must believe that the application of force is imminent, whereas an offence under s.5 is committed regardless of the actual belief of the victim. What matters is that the accused *intended* the victim to believe that the threat will be carried out.

PUNISHMENT ON CONVICTION

An offence under s.5 may be tried summarily or on indictment. On summary conviction the penalty is a maximum term of imprisonment of 12 months and/or a fine. On conviction on indictment, the penalty is a maximum term of imprisonment of 10 years and/or an unlimited fine.

SYRINGE OFFENCES

Sections 6, 7 and 8 of the 1997 Act create various offences involving the use of syringes. It is arguable that the inclusion of syringe offences in an Act originally intended to streamline the existing legislation defeats that purpose somewhat since the conduct prohibited by these provisions criminalises the *modus operandi* of carrying out activities that were not lawful to begin with. A comparison might be made with the various offences relating to the criminal damage to property contained in the Criminal Damage Act 1991, s.14(1) of which provides that where any of the offences contained in s.2 of that Act are committed by means of fire, this will be an aggravating factor which will attract a higher penalty. Arguably, the same could have been done in the Non-Fatal Offences Against the Person Act 1997 in respect of offences carried out using syringes.

Section 1 of the 1997 Act provides definitions relevant to the offences contained in the Act. "Syringe" is defined as including "any part of a syringe or a needle or any sharp instrument capable of piercing skin and passing onto or into a person blood or any fluid or substance resembling blood". "Contaminated blood" and "contaminated fluid" are also defined and a "contaminated syringe" is one which has "in it or on it contaminated blood or contaminated fluid".

Syringe Attacks

Section 6(1) provides that it is an offence to injure another by piercing the skin of that other person with a syringe or threatening to do so, intending the victim to believe that it is likely that he may become infected with a disease.

The actus reus is piercing the victim's skin with a syringe or threatening to do so.

The mens rea is intention or subjective recklessness in relation to the piercing or the threat thereof, coupled with intention or objective recklessness in relation to causing the victim to believe that he has been infected with a disease.

Punishment on conviction

This offence may be tried summarily or on indictment. On summary conviction the maximum penalty is a prison sentence of 12 months and/or a fine. On conviction on indictment the maximum penalty is a term of imprisonment of 10 years and/or an unlimited fine.

Spraying blood or a blood-like substance

Section 6(2) provides that it is an offence to pour, put or spray blood or a blood-like substance onto another person or to threaten to do so, intending the victim to believe that he may become infected with a disease.

The actus reus is spraying, putting or pouring blood or a blood-like substance on to the victim or threatening to do so. The mens rea for this offence is intention or recklessness in relation to the spraying, putting or pouring of blood or a blood-like substance onto the victim coupled with the intention of causing the victim to believe that he may become infected or being objectively reckless as to whether the victim will so believe.

PUNISHMENT ON CONVICTION

This offence may be tried summarily or on indictment. On summary conviction the maximum penalty is a prison sentence of 12 months and/or a fine. On conviction on indictment the maximum penalty is a term of imprisonment of 10 years and/or an unlimited fine.

TRANSFERRED INTENT

Section 6(3) provides that where in the course of committing an offence under either of the two previous sections, the actual victim is a third party, the doctrine of transferred intent will apply and the accused, if convicted, will be liable for the penalties provided for by the relevant sections.

STABBING WITH A CONTAMINATED SYRINGE

The offences contained in s.6(5) of the 1997 Act are aggravated forms of syringe offences. Section 6(5)(a) creates the offence of intentionally injuring another person by piercing his skin with a contaminated syringe.

The actus reus of the offence is stabbing with a contaminated syringe. The mens rea is the intention to pierce the skin with a syringe and knowledge of the fact that the syringe is contaminated.

Section 6(5)(b) makes it an offence to spray, put or pour contaminated blood onto another person. The actus reus is spraying, putting or pouring contaminated blood onto another person. It would appear, therefore, that to spray, pour or put contaminated fluid other than blood is an offence under s.6(2) but not under s.6(5). The mens rea is intention. Section 6(5)(c) provides for liability for the above offences arising out of transferred intent.

PUNISHMENT ON CONVICTION

Section 6 offences are tried on indictment and the maximum penalty is life imprisonment.

POSSESSION AND ABANDONMENT OF SYRINGES

Section 7 of the 1997 Act makes it an offence to possess a syringe or any blood in a container in any place with the intention of using it unlawfully to threaten or injure or intimidate another person. The section gives the Gardaí the power to stop, question and if necessary, search a person where they have reasonable grounds for believing that the person is in possession of the relevant articles with the intention of using them to injure, threaten or intimidate. Failure to co-operate with the Gardaí or obstruction of a garda is an offence under the section. It will be a defence to show that the syringe or container is in the possession of the accused for a valid reason.

Punishment on conviction

If tried summarily, the offence of failing to co-operate or obstruct a garda carries the maximum penalty of a term of imprisonment of six months and/or a fine.

The punishment for the substantive offence of possession on summary conviction is a maximum term of imprisonment of 12 months and/or a fine and on indictment the maximum penalty is a maximum sentence of seven years and/or an unlimited fine.

Section 8 of the Act deals with the placement or abandonment of syringes in any place where it is likely that injury will be caused and is caused, or where it is likely to frighten another person. It will be a defence to show that the person in possession of the syringe has a valid reason for such possession. Where the syringe is found in the defendant's normal place of residence and the defendant did not intentionally leave it in such a place or in a manner that it was likely to cause or did cause injury, this will also amount to a defence.

For an offence under s.8, on summary conviction the maximum penalty is a term of 12 months' imprisonment and/or a fine and on conviction on indictment the maximum penalty is a term of seven years and/or an unlimited fine. Where the accused is convicted on indictment of an offence under s.8(2) which is the intentional placement of a contaminated syringe in such a manner that it injures another, the maximum penalty is life imprisonment.

Coercion

Section 9 of the 1997 Act makes it an offence to engage in conduct with the objective of compelling the victim to do or to abstain from doing which the victim is lawfully entitled to do or abstain from doing. The prohibited conduct includes violence, intimidation, damage to property, watching or besetting certain places frequented by the victim and following the victim.

PUNISHMENT ON CONVICTION

On summary conviction the maximum penalty is a term of 12 months' imprisonment and/or a fine and on conviction on indictment the maximum penalty is a term of five years and/or an unlimited fine.

HARASSMENT

The offence of harassment is provided for by s.10 of the 1997 Act and occurs where the accused persistently follows, watches, besets or communicates with the victim. The type of behaviour envisaged by the section is that which is commonly referred to as "stalking". The offence is committed where the accused "by his or her acts intentionally or recklessly, seriously interferes with the other's peace or privacy and causes alarm, distress or harm to the other". The accused's actions may be intentional or reckless but the essence of the offence is the effect that those acts have on the victim. To this end the actions must be "such that a reasonable person would realise that the acts would seriously interfere with the other's peace and privacy, or cause alarm, distress or harm".

PUNISHMENT ON CONVICTION

On summary conviction the maximum penalty is a term of 12 months' imprisonment and/or a fine and on conviction on indictment the maximum penalty is a term of five years and/or an unlimited fine.

In addition, the court may impose a "non-contact" order. Section 10(3) permits the court to make such an order which is similar to an injunction in its effects. The order may prohibit certain conduct by the accused and failure to comply with the order is an offence in itself. The court, under s.10(5) is permitted to make such an order even where the accused has not been convicted of the offence, if it is satisfied that to do so would be in the interests of justice. In *The People (DPP) v Ramachandran* [2000] 2 I.R. 307 the accused had successfully appealed his conviction for harassment. Despite this, the court granted a "non-contact" order against him on the basis that his victims were in need of the court's protection.

DEMANDS FOR PAYMENT

Under s.11 of the 1997 Act, it is an offence to make demands for payment of a debt by methods which amount to misrepresentation, fraud or where the demands are intended to cause distress, alarm or humiliation to the victim by virtue of their frequency.

PUNISHMENT ON CONVICTION

This is a summary offence in respect of which a fine may be imposed.

POISONING

Section 12 provides that:

> a person shall be guilty of an offence if, knowing that the other does not consent to what is being done, he or she intentionally or recklessly administers to or causes to be taken by another a substance which he or she knows to be capable of interfering substantially with the other's bodily functions.

This includes a substance which could cause sleep or unconsciousness. The offence is committed either by directly administering a substance or causing the victim to take it. The offence therefore encompasses the "spiking" of drinks.

PUNISHMENT ON CONVICTION

On summary conviction the maximum penalty is a term of 12 months' imprisonment and/or a fine and on conviction on indictment the maximum penalty is a term of three years and/or an unlimited fine.

ENDANGERMENT

Section 13 provides that it is an offence for a person to intentionally or recklessly engage in conduct which creates a substantial risk of death or serious harm to another. In *The People (Director of Public Prosecutions) v McGrath*, unreported, Court of Criminal Appeal, May 27, 2004 and *The People (Director of Public Prosecutions) v Cagney*, unreported, Court of Criminal Appeal, May 27, 2004, convictions for endangerment were upheld. In *McGrath* the conduct in question was running after the victim and threatening him and in *Cagney* the defendant had struck the victim, causing him to fall and sustain injury. A separate offence of endangering traffic is contained in s.14. This offence is committed by intentionally placing any dangerous obstruction on a road, railway, street etc. being aware that injury to a person or damage to property may be caused by doing so or being reckless as to that fact.

PUNISHMENT ON CONVICTION

Both offences can be tried summarily or on indictment. On summary conviction the maximum penalty is a term of 12 months' imprisonment and/or a fine. On conviction on indictment the maximum penalty is a term of seven years and/or an unlimited fine.

FALSE IMPRISONMENT

The offence of false imprisonment is contained in s.15 of the 1997 Act which abolishes the common law offences of kidnapping and false imprisonment. Section 15(1) provides that a person shall be guilty of false imprisonment if he:

(a) takes or detains; or
(b) causes to be taken or detained; or
(c) otherwise restricts the personal liberty of another person.

The absence of consent on the part of the victim is a part of the actus reus of the offence. Section 15(2) provides that where the consent of the victim has been obtained by force, threat of force or deception, causing the victim to believe that he is legally obliged to consent, this will not amount to consent on the part of the victim.

PUNISHMENT ON CONVICTION

On summary conviction the maximum penalty is a term of 12 months' imprisonment and/or a fine and on conviction on indictment the maximum penalty is life imprisonment.

CHILD ABDUCTION

The issue of child abduction is covered by ss.16 and 17 of the 1997 Act. Section 16 makes it an offence for a parent or guardian to remove a child from the jurisdiction in violation of a court order or without the consent of the other parent or guardian(s). The accused will have a defence if he was unable to obtain the consent of any other parties whose consent should have been obtained, but acted in the belief that such consent would have been forthcoming. The accused can also rely on the defence that it was not his intention to deprive the other parent or guardian(s) of their rights.

Section 17 deals with the abduction of children by anyone other than the categories of persons covered by s.16. In this case there is no requirement that the child be removed from the jurisdiction. The essence of the offence is the intention to take or detain or cause to be taken or detained, a child younger than 16 years of age so that the child is removed from the custody of the person(s) who has or have control of the child. The accused will have a defence if he believes that the child is over the age of 16 years.

PUNISHMENT ON CONVICTION

Both offences can be tried summarily or on indictment but the Director of Public Prosecutions must consent to proceedings being taken in respect of the offence contained in s.16. On summary conviction the maximum penalty is a term of 12 months' imprisonment and/or a fine. On conviction on indictment the maximum penalty is a term of seven years and/or an unlimited fine.

Property Offences

12

This chapter looks at offences relating to criminal damage to property and at offences of dishonesty. The former is governed by the provisions of the Criminal Damage Act 1991 and the latter by those of the Criminal Justice (Theft and Fraud Offences) Act 2001.

THE CRIMINAL DAMAGE ACT 1991

The Criminal Damage Act 1991 repealed most of the pre-existing common law and statutory rules in relation to criminal damage to property. Section 2 of the 1991 Act creates three categories of offence: damaging property, damaging property with the intent to endanger life, and damaging property with intent to defraud. Offences involving threats to damage property, possession of anything with the intent to damage property and unauthorised accessing of data are also contained in ss.3 and 4 of the Act.

For the purposes of the Act, "property" is defined in s.1 as being either tangible or in the form of data. "Damage" is also defined in s.1 and includes destruction, defacing, rendering inoperable and also altering, corrupting and doing any act contributing to such alteration of data.

LAWFUL EXCUSE

Section 6 of the 1991 Act provides for the defence of lawful excuse where the defendant honestly believed that the owner of the property had or would have consented to the damage or, where the defendant believed that causing damage to property was necessary in order to protect himself or another person or property from immediate harm and, where the defendant believed that such action on his part was reasonable. This second application of the defence has been amended by s.21 of the Non-Fatal Offences Against the Person Act 1997 which requires that the actions of the defendant in damaging property have to be objectively reasonable in the circumstances.

Damaging Property

Section 2(1) of the 1991 Act provides that, "a person who without lawful excuse damages any property belonging to another intending to damage any such property or being reckless as to whether any such property would be damaged shall be guilty of an offence".

The actus reus is causing damage to someone else's property in the absence of a lawful excuse for doing so. The mens rea is intention or recklessness as to whether damage is caused.

The actual owner of the property need not be identified and further, s.7(2) provides that two presumptions arise in the context of damage to property. First, it is presumed that the property belongs to another person and secondly, it is presumed that the owner of the property did not consent to the damage caused. Both presumptions are rebuttable. The first presumption may be rebutted by showing that on the balance of probabilities, the property belongs to the defendant and the second presumption may be rebutted, again on the balance of probabilities that the owner consented to the damage.

Damaging Property with Intent to Endanger Life

This offence is contained in s.2(2) of the Act and is an aggravated form of the offence contained in the previous section. The aggravating factor is the intent to endanger life. The offence is committed where a person intentionally or recklessly, damages property and by doing so, intends to endanger the life of another person or is reckless as to whether the life of another person would be endangered.

The actus reus is essentially the same as that required in s.2(1) but differs in respect of the question of ownership of property, which is irrelevant to the offence under s.2(2). The mens rea has two aspects. First, the accused must intend to damage the property or be subjectively reckless as to whether such damage is caused. Secondly, the accused must intend to endanger life or be subjectively reckless as to whether life is endangered by the damage.

Damaging Property with Intent to Defraud

This offence is contained in s.2(3) which provides that, "a person who damages any property, whether belonging to himself or another with intent to defraud, is guilty of an offence".

The actus reus is damaging any property. In common with s.2(2), the issue of ownership of the property is irrelevant. The mens rea has two components. First, there must be the intent to damage the property. Secondly, the accused must intend by his actions to defraud others. Actual fraud need not be established.

For the purposes of all the offences under s.2, the relevant type of recklessness is subjective, with the caveat that the accused has foreseen the particular type of damage that was actually done. This is set out in s.2(6) of the Act.

ARSON

The common law offence of arson is abolished by s.14(1) of the 1991 Act and any statutory provisions which related to arson were repealed by s.15. Where damage under any offence contained in s.2 is caused by fire, such offence will be treated as arson, in accordance with s.2(4) of the Act.

PUNISHMENT ON CONVICTION

The offences contained in s.2 may be tried summarily or on indictment. On summary conviction the maximum penalty is a term or imprisonment of 12 months and/or a fine.

On conviction on indictment the maximum penalty for an offence under s.2 is a term of imprisonment of 10 years and/or a fine. Where a person is guilty of arson under ss.2(1) or 2(3) the maximum penalty is life imprisonment and/or an unlimited fine. The maximum penalty for the offence contained in s.2(2) is life imprisonment and/or an unlimited fine whether the offence is caused by arson or not.

THREATS TO DAMAGE PROPERTY

It is an offence under s.3 of the Act to threaten, without lawful excuse, to damage property owned by another person or to threaten to damage one's own property in circumstances where it would be likely to endanger the life of another person. The essence of the offence is the threat to damage property with the intention that the person to whom the threat is directed fears that it will be carried out. The threat might actually not be carried out but if it is carried out, the matter will be dealt with under the appropriate part(s) of s.2.

PUNISHMENT ON CONVICTION

On summary conviction the maximum penalty is a term of imprisonment of 12 months and/or a fine. On conviction on indictment, the maximum penalty is a sentence of 10 years' imprisonment and/or a fine.

POSSESSION WITH INTENT TO DAMAGE PROPERTY

Under s.4 of the 1991 Act, it is an offence to have in one's custody or under one's control, without lawful excuse, any implement that is intended to be used to commit an offence under s.2. Consequently, the prosecution must prove the possession element and the absence of any lawful excuse for the possession.

PUNISHMENT ON CONVICTION

On summary conviction the maximum penalty is a term of imprisonment of 12 months and/or a fine. On conviction on indictment, the maximum penalty is a sentence of 10 years' imprisonment and/or a fine.

UNAUTHORISED ACCESSING OF DATA

Section 5 of the 1991 Act creates the new offence of unauthorised accessing of data. This offence relates to the activity commonly referred to as "hacking". The offence is committed where a person within this jurisdiction "hacks" into a computer which is either within the State or outside it. It is also an offence for someone outside the State to use a computer to access any data kept within the State. It appears that the potential scope of this provision is very broad. The offence is committed where a computer is used with the intent to access data; it is not committed when data is actually accessed. Potentially, therefore an offence under s.5 is committed where the computer user even inadvertently types in the wrong password to access online material such as email.

PUNISHMENT ON CONVICTION

An offence under s.5 is a summary offence and carries a maximum penalty of three months' imprisonment and/or a fine.

THEFT AND DISHONESTY

THE CRIMINAL JUSTICE (THEFT AND FRAUD OFFENCES) ACT 2001

The Criminal Justice (Theft and Fraud Offences) Act 2001 repealed the Larceny Acts 1861, 1916 and 1990 and the Forgery Acts 1861 and 1913 which had previously governed the area of dishonesty. The 2001 Act consolidates and streamlines the offences contained in the older Acts and creates new offences relating to white-collar and computer crime.

THEFT

Section 4 provides that, "a person is guilty of theft if he or she dishonestly appropriates property without the consent of its owner and with the intention of depriving its owner of it".

The actus reus of theft is the appropriation of property without the consent of its owner. The mens rea is the intention to deprive the owner of the property.

DISHONESTY

"Dishonesty" is defined in s.2(1) as being "without a claim of right made in good faith". The test here is subjective. In *The People (Director of Public Prosecution) v O'Loughlin* [1979] I.R. 85 the Court of Criminal Appeal held that where there was an honest belief on the part of the accused as to whether he had a right to take property belonging to someone else, such belief would amount to a claim of right even where the belief turned out to be mistaken.

Under s.4(4) of the 2001 Act, the jury should have regard to the presence or absence of reasonable grounds for the belief.

APPROPRIATION

Section 4 differs significantly from the provision of the Larceny Act 1916 on the issue of appropriation. Whereas the 1916 Act required the accused to have taken and carried away the property, the 2001 Act provides that appropriation may occur even where the accused has possession of property belonging to another person. Appropriation, as defined in the 2001 Act, occurs where the accused engages in "usurping or adversely interfering with the proprietary rights of the owner".

It is not necessary, under s.4, to show that the accused intended to *permanently* deprive the owner of his property. This is another significant departure from the older legislation which required proof of an intention to permanently deprive.

CONSENT

Consent is a defence to a charge of theft. Section 4(2) of the 2001 Act provides that property is not appropriated without the consent of the owner in the following circumstances:

(i)   where the accused believes that he has, or would have, the consent of the owner, if the owner was aware of the appropriation of the property, or

(ii) where the accused believes that the owner cannot be ascertained by taking reasonable steps to do so.

The belief on the part of the accused is taken subjectively but under s.4(4), the jury is to have regard to the presence or absence of reasonable grounds for his belief. The defence is lost where consent is obtained by intimidation or fraud.

EXCEPTIONS TO THEFT

Section 5 deals with situations involving appropriation of property. Section 5(1) provides that theft does not occur in circumstances where property rights are transferred to a purchaser who buys the property in good faith and a defect in the title to the property is subsequently discovered.

Generally, land cannot be stolen and the term land includes anything that forms part of the land or anything that is affixed to the land.

The Act sets out three exceptions to the general rule that real property cannot be stolen. These are found in s.5(2) which provides that:

(1)   where the defendant has a duty imposed upon him by virtue of his being a trustee, a personal representative, the liquidator of a company or someone with power of attorney and he appropriates land in breach of his duty; or

(2)   where the defendant appropriates anything that forms part of the land by severing it or causing it to be severed, while not being in possession of the land; or

(3)   where the defendant possesses the land under a tenancy agreement or a lease and appropriates any fixture or structure.

Appropriation in either of these circumstances amounts to theft under the Act.

PUNISHMENT ON CONVICTION

Theft is an indictable offence which carries a maximum sentence of 10 years and/or an unlimited fine.

MAKING GAIN OR CAUSING LOSS BY DECEPTION

Sections 6, 7 and 8 of the Act deal with the offences of making gain or causing loss by deception, obtaining services by deception and making off without payment, respectively.

In accordance with s.6 of the Act, a person will be guilty of the offence of "making gain or causing loss by deception" where he dishonestly and with the intention of making a gain for himself or another person *or* causing loss to the victim, uses deception to induce the victim to act or to refrain from acting in a particular way. It must be established that the deception induced the victim to act or refrain from acting in a particular way. The section does not require proof of actual gain to the accused or to another person. Nor does it require proof of actual loss to the victim.

The offence of "obtaining services by deception" is provided for by s.7 of the Act. This offence is substantially similar to the offence under s.6 in terms of the conduct of the accused. The difference between the two offences is the outcome. Under s.7, it must be shown that the accused obtained services as a result of his deceptive conduct. Section 7(2) provides that a person obtains services where the victim is induced to confer some form of benefit on someone on the understanding that the benefit has been or will be paid for. The offence is also committed where the service conferred is a loan, in accordance with s.7(3) of the Act.

Section 8 provides for the offence of "making off without payment". The offence is committed where the accused, knowing that immediate payment is required for any goods or services, dishonestly makes off without paying with the intention of avoiding payment. The goods/services must not be unlawful and payment must be legally enforceable.

PUNISHMENT ON CONVICTION

These are all indictable offences and offences under ss.6 and 7 are punishable by a maximum term of imprisonment of five years and/or an unlimited fine. The offence of making off without payment under s.8 carries a maximum sentence of two years and/or a fine.

UNLAWFUL USE OF A COMPUTER

This is a new offence created by s.9 of the 2001 Act. It amplifies the provisions of s.5 of the Criminal Damage Act 1991, which created the offence of unauthorised accessing of data or "hacking". The type of action contemplated by s.9 is deemed to be more serious in nature than the "hacking" offence prohibited by s.5 of the 1991 Act and requires evidence that the accused made unlawful use of a computer either within the State or outside the State with the intention of making a gain for himself or causing a loss to another.

PUNISHMENT ON CONVICTION

This is an indictable offence which carries a maximum sentence of 10 years and/or an unlimited fine.

FALSE ACCOUNTING

Section 10 of the 2001 Act makes it an offence to destroy, deface, conceal or falsify accounts or documents pertaining to accounts, with the intention to make a gain or to cause a loss to another. It is also an offence under s.10 to make false or misleading accounts.

PUNISHMENT ON CONVICTION

False accounting is an indictable offence which carries a maximum sentence of 10 years and/or an unlimited fine.

BURGLARY

Section 12 provides that the offence of burglary is committed where a person enters a building as a trespasser with the intent to commit an arrestable offence, or being present as a trespasser, commits or attempts to commit an arrestable offence. An arrestable offence is defined in s.12(4) as being an offence "for which a person of full age and not previously convicted may be punished by imprisonment for a term of five years or by a more severe penalty".

The actus reus of burglary is entry on to premises as a trespasser to commit an arrestable offence *or* being on the premises as a trespasser and committing or attempting to commit such an offence.

There are two aspects to the mens rea: first, the accused must have the mens rea to enter the premises as a trespasser. It must be shown that he either intended to trespass or was reckless as to whether he was trespassing. Secondly, the accused must have the mens rea for the arrestable offence.

TRESPASS

Trespass is the unauthorised entry on to the property of another. It can happen in a number of ways:

(i) where the accused knowingly enters the premises without consent, or

(ii) where the accused has permission to be on the premises but then acts in a way that is not compatible with that permission, or

(iii) where the accused, having entered the premises innocently, subsequently realises that he is trespassing and fails to leave.

ENTRY

Section 12(2) provides the definition of "building" or "part of a building". For the purposes of the offence of burglary, entry does not necessarily have to mean full entry. In *R v Brown* [1985] Crim. L.R. 212 it was held that where the accused had partially entered a shop through a broken window this constituted a sufficient entry.

PUNISHMENT ON CONVICTION

Burglary is an indictable offence which carries a maximum term of imprisonment of 14 years and/or an unlimited fine.

AGGRAVATED BURGLARY

This offence is covered by s.13 of the Act and occurs where the offence of burglary (s.12) is committed by the accused, who has with him or has at the time, a firearm, imitation firearm, any weapon of offence or an explosive.

WEAPON

For the purposes of the Act, s.13(2) provides definitions of the types of weapons referred to in s.13(1).

A firearm is defined as including the following:

- a lethal firearm or any weapon capable of discharging a shot, bullet or other missile;
- airgun or any other weapon which incorporates a barrel and which is capable of firing metal or other slugs;
- a crossbow; or any type of gun which emits energy and causes shock or other disablement;

An *imitation firearm* is anything that is not a firearm, but which resembles one. A *weapon of offence* is any article with a sharp blade or point, any other article made or adapted to cause injury or incapacitation or any weapon of any description that is designed to emit any noxious substance.

The actus reus of aggravated burglary is essentially the same as with burglary but includes the possession of a weapon at the material time. The mens rea is the same as for burglary with the added requirement that the accused knew that he had a weapon.

PUNISHMENT ON CONVICTION

Aggravated burglary is an indictable offence which carries a maximum sentence of imprisonment for life.

ROBBERY

The offence of robbery is provided for by s.14 of the 2001 Act. A person commits robbery when he steals, and at the time or immediately before the stealing in order to do so, he or she uses force or puts or seeks to put any person in fear of being then and there subjected to force.

The actus reus of robbery has two separate components;

(i) stealing,
(ii) the use of force or threat of force at the time of the stealing or immediately prior to the stealing.

The use or threat of force need not be directed at the owner of the property. The use or threat of force must be immediately prior to or at the time of the stealing. It is not, therefore, robbery to take someone's property and *then* subject them to force or threaten to do so. In this instance, the appropriate charges are theft and assault. The essence of the offence of robbery is the use or threat of force in order to facilitate the stealing.

The mens rea also has two components; first, the accused must have the intention to steal and secondly, the accused must intend to use force or threaten to use force in order to steal.

PUNISHMENT ON CONVICTION

Robbery is an indictable offence which carries a maximum sentence of imprisonment for life.

Handling

Section 17 provides that the offence of handling is committed where a person, knowing that property is stolen, or reckless as to that fact, receives it or undertakes to assist in its retention, removal, disposal or realisation.

The actus reus of handling is receiving stolen property and assisting in its removal, disposal or realisation. The mens rea is knowledge of or recklessness as to whether the property is stolen.

Recklessness is defined by s.16(2) and can be established where the accused has ignored or disregarded a substantial risk that the property is stolen.

PUNISHMENT ON CONVICTION

Handling stolen property is tried on indictment and carries a maximum prison sentence of 10 years and/or an unlimited fine. The penalty imposed will not exceed that which applies to the principal offence.

POSSESSION OF STOLEN PROPERTY

Section 18 creates the offence of possession of stolen property. The offence is committed where a person without lawful authority or excuse, possesses stolen property, knowing that the property has been stolen, or reckless as to whether it has been stolen.

The actus reus is being in possession of stolen property. The mens rea is knowledge or recklessness as to whether the property is stolen.

Section 18(2) provides that where a person has in his possession stolen property in such circumstances that it is reasonable to conclude that the person knew the property to be stolen or was reckless as to the fact, it will be presumed that the person possessing such property knew that it was stolen. This presumption will be rebutted where there is a reasonable doubt as regards such knowledge or recklessness on the part of the person who has possession of the property.

PUNISHMENT ON CONVICTION

Possession of stolen property is tried on indictment and carries a maximum prison sentence of five years and/or an unlimited fine. The penalty imposed will not exceed that which applies to the principal offence.

Public Order Offences

13

Prior to the enactment of the Criminal Justice (Public Order) Act 1994 (as amended by the Criminal Justice (Public Order) Act 2003), the law governing this category of offence was contained in a number of different statutes most of which had been enacted in the 19th century. The 1994 Act sought to centralise these offences within one statute by repealing and updating most of the common law offences against public order. Of critical importance for the successful prosecution of the offences under the Act is the requirement that the conduct with which the accused is charged occurs in a public place as defined in the Act. This means that the location of the commission of the offence is part of what must be established by the prosecution. Where the prosecution fails or omits to discharge this element of the burden of proof, the accused must be acquitted.

A further issue to be considered is the potential vulnerability of certain sections of the Act to constitutional challenge. In particular, ss.5, 6 and 7 have been identified as potentially unconstitutional on the basis that they curtail a number of constitutionally protected rights namely, freedom of assembly and freedom of expression.

Many of the offences created by the Act prohibit conduct carried out with the intention to cause breach of the peace or where the accused is reckless as to whether a breach of the peace will occur. Breach of the peace was described in *The People (Attorney General) v Cunningham* [1932] I.R. 28 as an act which causes "reasonable alarm and apprehension to members of the public". More recently, the High Court was asked to determine whether a breach of the peace was a common law offence and if so, whether it was capable of being prosecuted in the District Court. The decision of the High Court in *Thorpe v Director of Public Prosecutions* [2007] I.R. 502 was that a person could be arrested and charged with breach of the peace under the Criminal Justice (Public Order) Act 1994 or, where the provisions of that Act do not apply, the person could be arrested and charged with breach of the peace at common law. The court also held that the term "breach of the peace" had two meanings at common law. The first of these is where the conduct of the accused causes reasonable alarm and apprehension to members of the public and the second meaning refers to situations where breach of the peace is not an offence. These occur where judicial discretion pursuant to s.54 of the Courts (Supplemental Provisions) Act 1961 is exercised in favour of binding a person over to keep the peace and be of good behaviour and where a common law power of arrest is being exercised by An Garda Síochána.

The remainder of this chapter deals with the main offences created by the 1994 Act (as amended).

INTOXICATION IN A PUBLIC PLACE

Section 4 of the Act makes it an offence for a person to be in a public place while intoxicated to such an extent as would give rise to a reasonable apprehension that he might endanger himself or some other person.

The actus reus of this offence is being intoxicated in a public place. The term "intoxicated" is defined in the Act as being under the intoxicating influence of any substance and a "public place" is defined as including any highway, any outdoor place to which members of the public have access, a cemetery or churchyard, premises to which the public have access or a right of access on payment or otherwise or any train, vessel or vehicle used as public transport.

The issue of mens rea does not really arise with this offence since it is committed by being in a public place whilst intoxicated to the extent that might give rise to the reasonable belief that a danger is posed to the defendant himself or to anyone else present. The "reasonable belief" requirement is an objective test. A prosecution under s.4 cannot be sustained if it is based solely on the fact that the accused was drunk in public. It must also be established that his behaviour gave rise to a reasonable fear that he was endangering himself or others.

Section 4(3) provides that if a Garda suspects, with reasonable cause that an offence under ss.4, 5 or 6 is being committed, the Garda may seize without warrant any bottle or container and its contents which is in the possession of the accused and which the Garda has reasonable cause to suspect contains an intoxicating substance.

PUNISHMENT ON CONVICTION

An offence under s.4 of the 1994 Act is a summary offence and the maximum penalty is a fine of €500. In addition to the confiscation powers of An Garda Síochána pursuant to s.4(3), s.3 of the Criminal Justice (Public Order) Act 2003 empowers the District Court to grant an Exclusion Order prohibiting the accused from entering or being in the vicinity of certain premises for a specified period of time. A new s.23B was inserted into the 1994 Act by s.184 of the Criminal Justice Act 2006 which permits the imposition of a fixed charge fine in lieu of criminal proceedings under s.4.

Disorderly Conduct in a Public Place

Section 5 of the 1994 Act provides that it is an offence to engage in offensive conduct in a public place between the hours of 12am and 7am or at any other time after a Garda requests that the behaviour in question ceases. The actus reus is engaging in offensive conduct in a public place between the relevant hours or at any time after a Garda has asked that the conduct ceases. The mens rea is intention or objective recklessness.

Offensive Conduct

Section 3 states that offensive conduct is any unreasonable behaviour, which having regard to all the circumstances, is likely to cause serious offence or annoyance to any person who is aware of such behaviour or who might reasonably be expected to be aware of it.

The purpose of s.5 is to outlaw behaviour that impacts adversely on the quality of life of others. The section is vaguely worded and it appears to create an offence of strict liability between the hours of 12am and 7am whereas the same conduct will not attract criminal liability at any other time unless the accused has refused to desist having been requested to do so by a Garda.

Punishment on conviction

An offence under s.5 of the 1994 Act is a summary offence and the maximum penalty is a fine of €1,000. The District Court may also impose an Exclusion Order pursuant to s.3 of the 2003 Act. A new s.23A was inserted into the 1994 Act by s.184 of the Criminal Justice Act 2006, which permits the imposition of a fixed charge fine in lieu of criminal proceedings under s.5.

Threatening, Abusive or Insulting Behaviour

Section 6 of the Act provides that an offence is committed by a person who uses threatening, abusive or insulting words or behaviour in a public place, with intent to provoke a breach of the peace or being reckless as to whether a breach of the peace may be occasioned. The offence created by s.6 is effectively an aggravated form of the offence under s.5 of the Act. The actus reus is being in a public place and using threatening, abusive or insulting words or behaving in a threatening, abusive or insulting manner. The mens rea is intention or objective recklessness as regards the conduct in question and also as to whether a breach of the peace will occur.

BREACH OF THE PEACE

A breach of the peace may occur where harm is caused to the person or property of an individual, or is likely to be caused or where an individual is put in fear of suffering harm through violence or some form of public disturbance.

PUNISHMENT ON CONVICTION

This is also a summary offence which carries a maximum prison sentence of three months and/or a fine of €1,000. A conviction for this offence may also result in the imposition of an Exclusion Order in accordance with s.3 of the 2003 Act.

OBSCENE DISPLAYS

Section 7(1) makes it an offence to distribute or display in public, any writing, sign or visible representation which is threatening, abusive, insulting or obscene with intent to provoke a breach of the peace or being reckless as to whether a breach of the peace may occur. The actus reus is the distribution or display in public of anything that is threatening, abusive, insulting or obscene. The mens rea is intention or objective recklessness as regards to the display or distribution of the material in question coupled with intention or objective recklessness as to whether a breach of the peace may be occasioned.

OBSCENITY

The test used to determine if something is obscene is whether the material in question tends to deprave and corrupt those whose minds are open to such immoral influences and into whose hands such a publication may fall. As a basis for imposing criminal liability, however, this is a test that could lead to arbitrariness, since what may be considered obscene by one person may well be regarded as an acceptable means of invoking the constitutionally protected right of freedom of expression by another. It is likely that the test to be applied is an objective one which would focus on what the reasonable person would consider to be obscene.

PUNISHMENT ON CONVICTION

An offence under s.7 is tried summarily and carries a maximum penalty of three months' imprisonment and/or a fine of €1,000 and may also result in the imposition of an Exclusion Order.

Wilful Obstruction

It is an offence under s.9 of the Act to wilfully prevent or interrupt the free movement of any person or vehicle, in a public place without lawful excuse.

The actus reus is the prevention or interruption of the free movement of any person or vehicle in a public place, without lawful authority. The mens rea is intention or wilfulness.

Punishment on Conviction

Wilful obstruction is a summary offence punishable by a fine not exceeding €400. An Exclusion Order may also be imposed.

Enforcement of the Act

Section 8 of the Act grants powers of enforcement to the Gardaí who may give an offender a direction either to desist from the conduct in question or to immediately leave the vicinity in a peaceable and orderly manner. In order to invoke s.8, the Garda must have formed the reasonable belief that an offence under ss.4, 5, 6, 7 or 9 has been committed or that the offender is loitering in a public place in circumstances which give rise to a reasonable apprehension that the safety of other people or property is under threat or that public peace may be disturbed. If the offender refuses or fails to comply with the direction of the Garda under s.8, without lawful excuse for so doing, an offence is thereby committed.

Punishment on Conviction

An offence under s.8 is tried summarily and carries a maximum penalty of six months' imprisonment and/or a fine of €1,000. The court may also impose an Exclusion Order.

Riot

Section 14 of the 1994 Act abolishes the common law offence of riot and creates a new statutory offence of the same name. Riot is the most serious form of public disturbance and occurs where 12 or more persons who are present together in any place, public or private, use, or threaten to use, unlawful violence for a common purpose and where the conduct of those persons, taken together is such as would cause a person of reasonable firmness, whether present or not, to fear for his safety or for that of another person. Where this occurs, each of the group who *uses violence* shall be guilty of riot.

Section 14(2) provides that it is immaterial whether the group of 12 or more persons use or threaten to use unlawful violence simultaneously at any place. The section further provides that the common purpose of the group may be inferred from their conduct and that it is not necessary that a person of reasonable firmness actually be present or be likely to be present. The effect or likely effect of the conduct of the group on this hypothetical person of reasonable firmness is sometimes referred to as "the notional bystander test". It should be noted that a common purpose is not the same as a conspiracy, which is an agreement to carry out an unlawful act. No prior agreement is necessary to establish a common purpose.

The actus reus of riot is the use or threat of use of unlawful violence, in any place, for a common purpose by a group of 12 or more people, present together and the actual use of violence by the defendant and the imagined reaction of a reasonable person.

The mens rea is intention or objective recklessness.

PUNISHMENT ON CONVICTION

Riot is an indictable offence which carries a maximum sentence of 10 years' imprisonment and/or an unlimited fine.

VIOLENT DISORDER

Section 15 of the 1994 Act creates the new offence of violent disorder. Section 15(5) states that references to the common law offence of riot or to the common law offence of riot and to tumult in previous enactments are to be construed as meaning violent disorder. Section 15(6) of the 1994 Act abolishes the common law offences of rout and unlawful assembly.

Essentially, the offence of violent disorder is a lesser species of riot and may be charged as an alternative offence. Section 15(1) provides that where three or more persons present together in any place, public or private, use or threaten to use unlawful violence and the conduct of the group of three or more when taken together would cause a person of reasonable firmness to fear for his safety or that of another person, then each of the group using or threatening to use unlawful violence will be guilty of violent disorder.

The actus reus of violent disorder is the use or threat of use of unlawful violence, in any place, by a group of three or more people, present together and the imagined reaction of a reasonable person. The mens rea is intention or subjective recklessness. This can be seen from the wording of s.15(3) which provides that, "a person shall not be convicted of the offence of violent disorder unless that person intends to use or threaten to use violence or is aware that his conduct may be violent or threaten violence".

Punishment on conviction

Violent disorder is tried on indictment and carries a maximum term of imprisonment of 10 years and/or an unlimited fine.

Affray

The common law offence of affray is abolished by s.16 of the 1994 Act which creates a new statutory offence of the same name. This offence in effect criminalises public brawling. Section 16(1) provides that where two or more persons use or threaten to use unlawful violence against each other in a place that is public or private or both and that their conduct, taken together, is such that a reasonable person would be caused to fear for his safety or for that of another person, each of the group will be guilty of affray.

The actus reus of affray is the use or threat of use of unlawful violence towards the other person(s) present in a place which is public, private or both and the reaction of a person of reasonable firmness to the conduct of the group, taken as a whole.

The mens rea is intention or subjective recklessness. Section 16(3) provides that, "a person shall not be convicted of the offence of affray unless that person intends to use or threaten to use violence or is aware that his conduct may be violent or threaten violence".

In *The People (Director of Public Prosecutions) v Reid and Kirwan* [2004] 1 I.R. 392 the Court of Criminal Appeal held that:

> "Unlike the offences of riot or violent disorder, the actual or threatened use of violence for the purpose of the new offence of affray must be violence 'towards each other'."

The facts of the case were that a group of people were fighting in a street and the Gardaí intervened in order to arrest them, whereupon the Gardaí were attacked. The first accused was charged with affray but there was no evidence adduced to show that he had been involved in the brawl but rather, that he had attacked the Gardaí. He was convicted of affray but the conviction was quashed on appeal on the basis that there was no evidence that he had used or threatened to use violence against any member of the group. The Court of Criminal Appeal stated that:

"That being so, it follows that there was no prima facie case against the first accused on the charge of affray and that count should have been withdrawn from the jury."

For the purpose of affray, the threat of violence by words alone will not suffice; there must be some physical manifestation of the threat. It appears from the wording of the section that liability is imposed on each of the group even where unlawful violence is only used or threatened by one person. This problem was discussed by the Court of Criminal Appeal in *Reid and Kirwan*, where Hardiman J. stated that, "if that is the correct construction of the section, then, obviously, it raises questions of a far reaching nature".

PUNISHMENT ON CONVICTION

The offence of affray may be tried summarily or on indictment. The maximum penalty on conviction on indictment for the offence of affray is a term of imprisonment of up to five years and/or an unlimited fine with lesser penalties available on summary conviction.

ASSAULT WITH INTENT

Section 18 of the 1994 Act contains the offence of assault with intent to cause bodily harm or intent to commit an indictable offence. The offence is a species of aggravated assault. Given that the offence of common law assault has been abolished by the Non-Fatal Offences Against the Person Act 1997 and that the 1994 Act does not provide a definition for assault for the purposes of s.18, it must be supposed that an assault under this section is the same as an assault under s.2 of the Non-Fatal Offences Against the Person Act 1997, since the latter Act does not appear to have repealed the assault offences contained in the 1994 Act.

The actus reus is assault to commit bodily harm or to commit an arrestable offence.

The mens rea is the intention to commit the assault and the intention to commit bodily harm or an arrestable offence. It appears that recklessness would not suffice for this offence.

PUNISHMENT ON CONVICTION

The maximum penalty that can be imposed for this offence is a term of imprisonment of up to five years and/or an unlimited fine.

Assault or Obstruction of a Peace Officer

Section 38 of the Offences against the Person Act 1861 is repealed by s.19 of the Criminal Justice (Public Order) Act 1994, which creates a number of offences relating to obstruction of and assaults on a peace officer. The original definition of "peace officer", for the purposes of the section, was a member of the Garda Síochána, a member of the Defence Forces or a prison officer. This definition has now been extended pursuant to s.185 of the Criminal Justice Act 2006 to include ambulance, fire brigade personnel and personnel working in hospital Accident and Emergency Departments. The section also provides that an offence is committed where an assault is carried out against any person assisting a peace officer or where such person is obstructed whilst assisting a peace officer.

Section 19(1) provides that any person who does any of the following commits an offence:

(a) assaults a peace officer acting in the execution of the peace officer's duty, knowing that he is, or being reckless as to whether he is, a peace officer acting in the execution of his duty, or
(b) assaults any other person acting in the aid of a peace officer, or
(c) assaults any other person with intent to resist or prevent the lawful apprehension or detention of himself or any other person for any offence,

The actus reus for s.19(1)(a) is an assault on a peace officer acting in the execution of his duty. The mens rea is intention or subjective recklessness as outlined in *The People (Director of Public Prosecutions) v Murray* [1977] I.R. 360.

The actus reus for s.19(1)(b) is assault on a person assisting a peace officer. The provision does not state that in this instance the peace officer must be acting "in the execution of his duty" but is more than likely intended to mean this. The mens rea for assault is intention or recklessness. The wording of the subsection is unclear as to the mens rea required for the rest of the actus reus. It would also seem that following *Murray*, the accused must have some knowledge as to the fact that the victim is assisting a peace officer or be subjectively reckless in this regard and that the peace officer is acting, as per s.19(1)(a) "in the execution of his duty".

The actus reus of s.19(1)(c) is assault in order to prevent lawful apprehension or detention of the defendant or any other person. The mens rea is intention or recklessness with regard to the assault. Additionally there must be intention as regards the resistance to, or prevention of, lawful apprehension or detention. This appears to require knowledge on the part of the defendant as regards the lawful apprehension or detention, which it appears, does not necessarily have to be effected by a peace officer.

PUNISHMENT ON CONVICTION

This offence may be tried summarily at the election of the defendant and in that instance carries a maximum penalty of 12 months' imprisonment and/or a fine of up to €5,000. If tried on indictment, the maximum penalty on conviction is a term of imprisonment of five years and/or an unlimited fine.

Section 19(3) provides that any person who resists or wilfully obstructs a peace officer in the execution of his duty or a person assisting a peace officer in the execution of his duty, knowing or being reckless to whether he is a peace officer in the execution of his duty will have committed an offence by so doing.

The actus reus is resisting or wilfully obstructing a peace officer or anyone assisting a peace officer in the execution of his duty. The mens rea is intention or subjective recklessness. It might be argued that the vagueness inherent in ss.19(1)(b) and 19(1)(c) would have been largely avoided had those sections been drafted in similar terms.

For an offence under s.19(3), on summary conviction the maximum penalty is a term of six months' imprisonment and/or a fine of €2,500.

Offences Against the State

There are numerous pieces of legislation that deal with conduct which is deemed to be detrimental to the interests of the State, the gravest of which is treason. For the most part, offences of this nature are contained in the Offences Against the State Act 1939, which has been amended on several occasions. Other offences are located in the Official Secrets Act 1963. This chapter deals with the most important of these statutory provisions.

TREASON

Article 39 of Bunreacht na hÉireann provides that:

> Treason shall consist only in levying war against the State or assisting any state or person or inciting or conspiring with any person to levy war against the State, or attempting in force of arms or other violent means to overturn the organs of government established in this Constitution, or taking part or being concerned in or inciting or conspiring with any person to make or to take part or be concerned in any such attempt.

Article 39 is amplified by the provisions of the Treason Act 1939. Prior to the passing of the Criminal Justice Act 1990, the penalty for treason was death although the sentence was usually commuted to life imprisonment by the President in accordance with Art.13.6 of Bunreacht na hÉireann. The Criminal Justice Act 1964 abolished the death penalty for most offences with the exception of certain offences under the Offences Against the State Act 1939, certain military law offences, capital murder and treason. Ireland's obligations under various Conventions and membership of the European Union required total abolition of the death penalty and this came about with the enactment of the Criminal Justice Act 1990. All references to the death penalty in Bunreacht na hÉireann were removed following the Twenty-First Amendment that was passed by referendum in 2001.

Section 2 of the Criminal Justice Act 1990 now provides that treason is an offence punishable by imprisonment for life. Section 4 of the Act provides that a minimum of 40 years be served, provided the accused is an adult.

CRIMINAL LAW

SEDITION

Article 40.6.1 of Bunreacht na hÉireann grants protection to numerous rights, among which is freedom of expression. The Article also provides that this right may be subject to limitation on various grounds, among which are the protection of public order and the authority of the State. The Article goes on to declare that the publication or the utterance of seditious matter is an offence which shall be punishable by law. Sedition may be described as being conduct which goes beyond mere criticism of government and which is aimed at undermining the authority of the State but falls short of treason. Sedition therefore, can be seen as a lesser species of treason. Section 10(1)(c) of the Offences Against the State Act 1939 provides that it is an offence to set up in type, print, send by post, distribute, sell or offer for sale any document which is or contains or includes a seditious document.

THE OFFICIAL SECRETS ACT 1963

The Official Secrets Act 1963 contains three categories of offences. Part II of the Act deals with Official Information. Section 4 of the Act prohibits the disclosure of official information without authorisation to do so. Section 6 prohibits the retention of any official document or official information in the absence of any right or duty to do so.

Part III of the Act deals with offences that involve the communication of information where to do so would be prejudicial to the safety or preservation of the State.

Section 9 provides that a person shall not, in any manner prejudicial or contrary to the safety or preservation of the State, obtain, record, communicate or publish or have possession of any document or record of any of the following:

(i) the number, description, armament, equipment, disposition, movement or condition of any of the Defence Forces or of any of the vessels or aircraft belonging to the State,

(ii) any operations or projected operations of any of the Defence Forces or of the Garda Síochána or of any of the vessels or aircraft belonging to the State,

(iii) any measures for the defence or fortification of any place on behalf of the State,

(iv) munitions of war, or

(v) any other matter whatsoever information as to which would or might be prejudicial to the safety or preservation of the State.

It will be a defence to show that the defendant's conduct was authorised by the relevant Minister, someone acting on the Minister's behalf or as pursuant to his duties as a holder of public office. Section 10 of the Act provides that where the accused is charged with an offence under s.9 and he has been in communication with or attempted to communicate, whether inside or outside the State, with a foreign agent or a member of an unlawful organisation, such communication will be evidence that his action was prejudicial to the interests of the State. Where the accused has visited the address of the foreign agent or a member of an unlawful organisation or has consorted or associated with such individuals or where the address of such individuals is found in the possession of the accused, this will constitute evidence of communication between the accused and the foreign agent or member of an unlawful organisation. The onus of proof then shifts to the accused who must prove the contrary.

The provision further defines a "foreign agent" and a "member of an unlawful organisation" and includes people who are reasonably suspected to be such.

Section 13 of the Act declares that a person who contravenes or attempts to contravene any of the provisions of the Act is liable on summary conviction to a maximum sentence of six months and/or a fine. Offences under s.9 and those contained in Pt II of the Act may be tried on indictment where, upon conviction, the maximum penalty is a term of imprisonment of seven years.

THE OFFENCES AGAINST THE STATE ACTS 1939–1998

The Offences Against the State Act 1939 is the principal piece of legislation dealing with offences against the State. The purpose of the Act, as originally enacted, was to suppress activity deemed to be subversive in nature and, to this end, the Act contains some fairly radical, if not utterly draconian measures. The Act is divided into five parts with only the first three being intended to be permanent. Part V of the Act provides for the establishment of the Special Criminal Court, the jurisdiction of which has already been discussed. Section 30 of the Act deals with the arrest and detention of suspected persons and is one of the few statutory measures that allow for detention for the purposes of questioning. The constitutionality of s.30 was upheld by the Supreme Court in *The People (DPP) v Quilligan* [1987] I.L.R.M. 606. Although there are 59 sections in the Act in total, relatively few of these are used with any great frequency. These are as follows:

Section 18

The purpose of s.18 of the 1939 Act is to provide justificatory grounds for the suppression of organisations which are deemed to be unlawful. An organisation may be deemed unlawful if it is one that:

(a) engages in, promotes, encourages, or advocates the commission of treason or any activity of a treasonable nature, or

(b) advocates, encourages, or attempts the procuring by force, violence, or other unconstitutional means of an alteration of the Constitution, or

(c) raises or maintains or attempts to raise or maintain a military or armed force in contravention of the Constitution or without constitutional authority, or

(d) engages in, promotes, encourages, or advocates the commission of any criminal offence or the obstruction of or interference with the administration of justice or the enforcement of the law, or

(e) engages in, promotes, encourages, or advocates the attainment of any particular object, lawful or unlawful, by violent, criminal, or other unlawful means, or

(f) promotes, encourages, or advocates the non-payment of moneys payable to the Central Fund or any other public fund or the non-payment of local taxation,

shall be an unlawful organisation within the meaning and for the purposes of this Act, and this Act shall apply and have effect in relation to such organisation accordingly.

Section 19

The Government is not required to issue a declaration to the effect that a particular organisation is an unlawful one for the purposes of the Act. However, s.19 provides that the Government may make a Suppression Order with regard to any organisation where it is of the opinion that the organisation in question is an unlawful one. The Suppression Order is conclusive evidence that the organisation named within it is an unlawful organisation.

Section 20

A member of the organisation in respect of which the Suppression Order is made, may under s.20 of the Act, apply to either the High Court or the Attorney General for what is referred to in the Act as a "declaration of legality". This application must be made within 30 days of the making of the Suppression Order and an appeal from the decision lies to the Supreme Court. If the declaration of legality is granted, the Suppression Order "shall forthwith become null and void". No action carried out pursuant to the Suppression Order prior to the granting of the declaration of legality will be affected by this. If the declaration is not granted, and an appeal against this decision to the Supreme Court is not successful, neither the fact that the application was made nor any admissions or statements made by the applicant, whether orally or on affidavit, in the course of the application, may be used in evidence for the purposes of any subsequent prosecution of the applicant on charges of membership of the unlawful organisation.

SECTION 52

Section 52 of the Act provides that where a suspect is detained pursuant to s.30 of the Act, the Gardaí may demand that he gives a full account of his movements and actions within a specified period and all information in his possession regarding the commission or intended commission of any offence under the Act, or any scheduled offence, by another person. Failure or refusal to give such an account or information as demanded is an offence under s.52(2) of the Act, which attracts a maximum penalty of six months' imprisonment. This provision has also been challenged on the grounds that it infringes the right to silence, a right protected by Bunreacht na hÉireann as being part and parcel of the right under Art.38 to a trial "in due course of law". In *Heaney v Ireland* [1996] 1 I.R. 580 the Supreme Court upheld the section on the basis that curtailment of the right to silence was a proportionate means of achieving the objective of the Offences Against the State Act 1939.

THE OFFENCES AGAINST THE STATE (AMENDMENT) ACT 1972

The 1939 Act has been amended on a number of occasions and one noteworthy example of such amendment is to be found in s.3 of the Offences Against the State (Amendment) Act 1972 which provides that any statements made orally or in writing or otherwise or by any conduct, by the accused which imply or lead to the reasonable inference that he is a member of an unlawful organisation shall be evidence of such membership.

"Conduct" is inclusive of a failure on the part of the accused to deny published reports of such membership. The section provides that such failure to deny published reports of membership shall not on its own be conclusive evidence of membership. Section 3(2) of the 1972 Act further provides that where a member of the Garda Síochána, not below the rank of Chief Superintendent states in evidence that he is of the belief that the accused is a member of an unlawful organisation, that statement shall be evidence of such membership.

Section 3(2) was challenged in *O'Leary v Attorney General* [1993] 1 I.R. 102 on the grounds that it was an infringement of the presumption of innocence. The accused was found in possession of Republican posters and was convicted of membership of an unlawful organisation, the posters being deemed to have been "incriminating documents".

The challenge failed on the basis that if the court agreed that the evidence did not establish the accused's guilt beyond reasonable doubt he was entitled to be acquitted of the charge. In *The People (Director of Public Prosecutions) v Ferguson*, unreported, Court of Criminal Appeal, October 27, 1975, the Court of Criminal Appeal held that the statement of the Chief Superintendent as to his belief regarding the defendant's membership of an unlawful organisation was not conclusive in and of itself as regards the charge against the accused. O'Higgins C.J. stated that where the accused denied the charge on oath "the value and cogency to be attached the expression of belief ... would be obviously very much diminished". In *The People (Director of Public Prosecutions) v Mulligan*, unreported, Court of Criminal Appeal, May 17, 2004, Keane C.J. stated that, "the weight to be given to that evidence [the belief of the Chief Superintendent] was entirely a matter for the court of trial." More recently, the Supreme Court upheld s.3 in *The People (Director of Public Prosecutions) v Kelly* [2006] IESC 20 notwithstanding the court's recognition of what it referred to as the "inherent limitation on cross-examination" contained in the section.

THE OFFENCES AGAINST THE STATE (AMENDMENT) ACT 1998

Further amendments were made to the 1939 Act with the enactment, following the Omagh Bombing, of the Offences Against the State (Amendment) Act 1998. The most significant of these are as follows:

SECTION 2

Section 2 of the 1998 Act provides that where evidence is given in the course of proceedings under s.21 of the 1939 Act that the accused failed to answer any question material to the investigation of the offence, before or after being charged, the court is entitled to draw "such inferences from the failure as appear proper". Such failure may then be treated as corroborative of any other evidence but this will not be sufficient in and of itself for the purposes of conviction.

Section 6

Section 6 of the 1998 Act creates the new offence of directing an unlawful organisation, an offence punishable by life imprisonment. The section provides that it is an offence to direct the activities of any unlawful organisation, at any level of that organisation's structure, which is the subject of a Suppression Order pursuant to s.19 of the 1939 Act.

Section 10

Section 10 provides for the extension of the maximum period of detention pursuant to s.30 of the 1939 Act. Since the passing of the 1998 Act, the maximum period of detention under s.30 is 72 hours.

Organised Crime

Since the first edition of this book, there have been a number of significant legislative measures enacted to deal with the issue of organised crime, which, in popular perception has become more prevalent in recent years. Among the relatively recent statutory initiatives introduced is the Criminal Justice (Terrorist Offences) Act 2005 which provides for the European Arrest Warrant and permits the retention of data for up to three years for the purpose of the investigation of crime or for the security of the State, the Proceeds of Crime Acts 1996 and 2005, and the Criminal Assets Bureau Act 1996 to name but a few. The Criminal Justice Act 2006 provides for extended powers in the context of search warrants, seizure of goods and an extension of detention periods. Section 11 of the Criminal Justice Act 2007 provides that a person released on bail may be electronically monitored. In the context of organised or so-called "gangland" crime, two pieces of legislation are of significant importance and the remainder of this chapter deals with these.

PART VII OF THE CRIMINAL JUSTICE ACT 2006

Part VII of the 2006 Act deals with "organised crime". Section 70 of the 2006 Act set out a number of definitions for the purposes of Pt VII. In particular, the term "criminal organisation" was defined as being a structured group of three or more people, acting in concert, which has been established over a period of time and which has, as its main objective, the commission or facilitation of one or more serious offences in order to obtain, directly or indirectly, a financial or other material benefit. A "serious offence" in the context of Pt VII of the Act, is one which carries a potential sentence of four years' imprisonment. The group of three or more people must be a "structured group", defined in Pt VII as one which is not randomly formed for the purpose of committing a single offence and which does not need to have formally defined roles for its members, continuity of membership or a developed structure.

CONSPIRACY

Section 71 creates the statutory offence of conspiracy in the context of organised crime. The offence, which may be committed within or outside the

State occurs where a person conspires with one or more others to carry out a act within the State or outside, that constitutes or would constitute a serious offence within the State. Any person found guilty of conspiracy is liable to the same penalty as the principle offender.

ORGANISED CRIME

Section 72 provides that it is an offence for a person to knowingly participate in or contribute to the activities of a criminal organisation with the objective of enabling the criminal organisation to commit a serious offence in the State or outside the State. The mens rea is the intention to participate in the knowledge that by doing so, the accused is assisting a criminal organisation. In the event that the serious offence is to be committed outside the State, no offence of conspiracy will have been committed unless the accused participated or contributed within the State or on a State-registered vessel or aircraft. The prosecution does not have to prove that a serious offence was committed by the criminal organisation either within or outside the State. Nor must it be established that the accused, through his participation or contribution, actually enabled the criminal organisation or even that the accused knew the specific nature of the offence to be committed. A court, in determining whether the accused was part of a conspiracy, is permitted to consider whether the accused used a name, symbol, word or any other representation that is associated with the criminal organisation or from which the criminal organisation may be identified. The court may also consider whether the accused receives any benefit from the criminal organisation. The penalty for the offence of conspiracy under s.72 is a maximum term of imprisonment of five years and/or an unlimited fine.

COMMITTING AN OFFENCE FOR A CRIMINAL ORGANISATION

Section 73 of the Act provides that a person who commits a serious offence for the benefit of, at the direction of, or in association with, a criminal organisation is guilty of an offence. The person need not be a member of the criminal organisation or even know any of its members. The penalty for this offence is a maximum term of imprisonment of 10 years and/or an unlimited fine.

The Criminal Justice (Amendment) Act 2009

Significant amendments were made to Pt VII of the Criminal Justice Act 2006 with the enactment of the Criminal Justice (Amendment) Act 2009. The stated purpose of the Act is to, inter alia, provide for "additional measures with respect to combating organised crime and, in particular, with respect to countering the increased levels of violence towards, and intimidation of, members of the public perpetrated by criminal organisations ...". Prior to its enactment, a number of concerns were raised about the potential impact of the provisions of the Bill on constitutional and civil rights. The Council of State was convened by the President in order to obtain advice on the potential referral of the Bill to the Supreme Court pursuant to Art.26 of Bunreacht na hÉireann, but ultimately, the Bill was not referred and was signed into law. Thus, the Act enjoys the presumption of constitutionality.

Section 3 of the Act extends the definition of "criminal organisation" contained in the 2006 Act. For the purposes of the 2009 Act and Pt VII of the 2006 Act, a "criminal organisation" is now defined as:

> ... a structured group, however organised, that has as its main purpose or activity the commission of a serious offence.

A "structured group" is one which meets the following criteria:

(1) It must have three or more people;
(2) It must not have been randomly formed for the immediate commission of a single offence;
(3) The involvement of two or more of these individuals is with a view to their acting in concert.

The structured group need not have any formal rules or membership or any formal roles for any of its members. There need be no hierarchical or leadership structure and it is not necessary that the members of the group themselves directly participate in the commission of criminal offences.

Section 5 of the 2009 Act inserts a new provision into s.71 of the 2006 Act. The newly inserted provision creates the offence of "directing a criminal organisation". The offence is committed where the accused directs the activities of a criminal organisation at any level. Pursuant to the Act, a person "directs" an organisation where he controls or supervises activities or gives an order, or issues guidance or a request with respect to the activities of the organisation. The maximum penalty on conviction for the offence under s.5 is life imprisonment. Further, the section provides that any statement or conduct by the accused which leads to a reasonable inference of his guilt is admissible

ORGANISED CRIME

as evidence of his guilt. The court may also have regard to a number of other factors in determining whether the accused has committed an offence under s.5. These factors are set out in s.5(4) and include any evidence of a pattern of behaviour by the accused which is consistent with the directing of a criminal organisation or the possession by the accused of any articles, documents or records which would give rise to a reasonable suspicion of guilt under s.5.

A further offence of participation in or contributing to criminal activities is created by s.6 of the 2009 Act, which amends the 2006 Act by the substitution of a new s.72. The offence under s.6 is committed where the accused participates in or contributes to *any* activity with the intention of enhancing the capability of the criminal organisation or any of its members to commit a serious offence or to facilitate the commission of a serious criminal offence by the organisation or any of its members *or* being reckless as to whether his conduct could enhance the ability of the organisation to commit a serious offence or facilitate in the commission of a serious offence by the organisation or its members. The activity engaged in by the accused need not be a criminal offence; in other words, the section criminalises any activity on the part of the accused which is carried out with the intention of assisting the criminal organisation to commit a serious offence. In order to convict the accused for an offence under s.6, it must be shown that he knew of the existence of the organisation when he participated in or contributed to its activities.

The prosecution need not prove that the criminal organisation committed or any of its members actually committed a serious offence within or outside the jurisdiction. Nor must the prosecution establish that the conduct of the accused actually enhanced the ability of the organisation to commit a serious offence or that it facilitated the commission of a serious offence by the criminal organisation. The maximum penalty for an offence under s.6 is a term of imprisonment of up to 15 years and/or an unlimited fine. The court may consider any relevant factor including whether the accused uses a name, word, symbol or other representation that identifies the criminal organisation or is associated with it. Section 6 of the 2009 Act also contains a Table of incriminating articles including, balaclavas, boiler suits, any means of disguise or impersonation (including any article of Garda uniform or equipment), firearms, knives, any implement for burglary or gaining access to any premises, plans of premises, controlled drugs within the meaning of the Misuse of Drugs Act 1977, substantial amounts of cash or currency, false vehicle registration plates, or any other article which may be prescribed for the purposes of s.6. The significance of the Table of articles is as follows: the possession by the accused of any of these articles can be a factor from which the intention of the accused, in relation to the offence, may be inferred.

SCHEDULED OFFENCES

Section 8 of the 2009 Act provides that certain offences are to be included in the list of offences scheduled to the Offences Against the State Acts 1939–1998. These include the offences pertaining to criminal organisations contained in Pt VII of the Criminal Justice Act 2006 and those created by ss.5 and 6 of the Criminal Justice (Amendment) Act 2009. The effect of scheduling an offence to the Offences Against the State Acts is that those offences are automatically sent for trial in the Special Criminal Court which sits without a jury. To that end, s.8 provides that:

> "It is hereby declared that the ordinary courts are inadequate to secure the effective administration of justice and the preservation of public peace and order in relation to [certain provisions of Pt VII of the 2006 Act]."

As noted previously, Art.38.5 of Bunreacht na hÉireann permits derogation from the general right to trial by jury for serious offences in certain, specified circumstances, one of which being where there is a declaration that the ordinary courts are inadequate to secure the administration of justice. Section 8 appears to foreclose any challenge to the use of the Special Criminal Court for the trial of certain "gangland" offences. The wording of the relevant sections which create offences pertaining to criminal organisations has been the subject of much commentary, a lot of which centres around the vague wording of the offences. In that regard, the statement of the Supreme Court in *King v Attorney General* [1981] I.R. 233 is instructive. In that case, the Supreme Court held that a section of the Vagancy Act 1824 was unconstitutional on grounds of vagueness having been described by the Supreme Court as:

> "... so arbitrary, so vague, so difficult to rebut ... and so generally at variance with both the explicit and implicit characteristics and limitations of the criminal law as to the onus of proof and mode of proof, that it is not so much a question of ruling unconstitutional the type of offence we are now considering as identifying the particular constitutional provisions with which such an offence is at variance."

Inchoate Offences

16

This category of offences covers attempts, conspiracy and incitement. Although sometimes referred to as incomplete offences, this is a misnomer since inchoate offences are complete offences in themselves. All that is meant by the term "incomplete" in this context is that the substantive offence that was the subject of the attempt, conspiracy or incitement may not have been carried out. This in no way reduces liability in respect of the inchoate offences. All three forms of inchoate offence are creatures of common law in Ireland, neither one having been given statutory expression. A person convicted of an attempt may be punished as though the substantive offence had actually been completed.

ATTEMPT

The actus reus of an attempt is some conduct on the part of the accused which is sufficiently proximate to the intended offence to incur liability. If the conduct of the accused is too remote or is merely preparatory in nature, the accused will not be convicted. In *R v Eagleton* (1855) 169 E.R. 66 the accused was convicted of obtaining money by false pretences. The basic principles of the offence of attempt were outlined by the court and may be summarised as follows:

(i)   Intention is not a sufficient basis upon which to establish the offence.
(ii) There must be some act(s) accompanying the intention.
(iii) The act(s) must be in some way immediately connected to the substantive offence.

The Court of Criminal Appeal ruled along similar lines in *The People (Attorney General) v Thornton* [1952] I.R. 91 defining the term "attempt" as:

"... an act done by the accused with a specific intent to commit a particular crime; it must go beyond mere preparation and must be a direct movement towards the commission after the preparations have been made".

Two distinct and competing approaches to establishing the actus reus of attempt have evolved from *Eagleton*, namely the "proximate act" and the "last act" approaches. The former is premised on the requirement that the conduct of the accused is not too remote whereas the latter approach requires that the accused has committed the final act that is required in order to enable the commission of the substantive offence being attempted. Essentially, both approaches are concerned with setting the appropriate threshold which must be reached before liability for attempt can be imposed.

The leading Irish case on attempt is *The People (Attorney General) v Sullivan* [1964] I.R. 169 where the Supreme Court stated that the decisive factor in determining whether the offence of attempt had been committed was whether the actions of the accused were "merely as a preparation for the commission of offences or whether they constituted acts sufficiently proximate to amount to attempts to commit the substantive offences."

PROXIMITY

The difficulty of ascertaining the exact point at which an act has gone beyond mere preparation and becomes sufficiently proximate to incur liability is not altogether clear, and will largely depend on the facts of each case. In *The People (Attorney General) v England* [1947] 1 Frewen 81, the Court of Criminal Appeal held that words alone could not amount to an attempt and that some positive action was required. In *The People (Attorney General) v Sullivan* [1964] I.R. 169 the accused, a midwife, was charged with attempting to obtain money by false pretences. The basis of the allegation was that she had devised a scheme whereby she would receive payments in respect of fictitious patients. An additional allowance was payable when the number of patients she treated went above 25. The accused duly submitted claim forms but it was not clear whether the fictitious patients were among the first 25. The Supreme Court held that for an act to be considered an attempt, it must be sufficiently proximate to the commission of the substantive offence and that where an act is the first in a series of similar actions, all carried out in furtherance of the commission of an offence, each action could be deemed sufficiently proximate to result in a conviction for attempt.

Another approach that has been used in determining proximity is the so-called "last act theory". This approach is posited on the notion that where the accused has committed the last act before the substantive offence is committed, he is guilty of attempt. In *DPP v Stonehouse* [1977] 2 All E.R. 909 the accused was charged with and convicted of attempting to enable another to obtain money. The defendant, a former government minister, took out a number of life insurance policies and then faked his own death. He was subsequently discovered alive, although the insurance had not been claimed by his wife, who was not part of the scam and believed the accused to be dead. The House of Lords upheld his conviction for attempting to commit the offence on the basis that he had done everything he could possibly have done to enable the offence to be committed, or in the words of Lord Diplock, "the offender must have crossed the Rubicon and burnt his boats".

The mens rea for all attempts is the intention to commit the substantive offence. This is the case even where recklessness would be sufficient mens rea for the substantive offence. In *The People (Director of Public Prosecutions) v Douglas and Hayes* [1985] I.L.R.M. 25, the court held that the defendants could be convicted of shooting with intent to commit murder, an offence under the Offences Against the Person Act 1861, where it could be shown that they had an intent to kill. If the intent to kill could not be proved, the defendants could not be convicted. The relevant section of the 1861 Act provided for a species of attempted murder. The modern law on attempted murder requires that the accused intended to kill; an intention to seriously injure will not suffice, even though the substantive offence of murder can be proven where the accused intends to seriously injure the victim.

IMPOSSIBILITY

If the accused attempts to do something that is either legally or physically impossible, he cannot be convicted of attempt. Impossibility therefore, is a defence to a charge of attempt. In *Houghton v Smith* [1975] A.C. 476, it was held that the accused could not be convicted of handling stolen goods where the goods were not in fact stolen.

Similarly, if something is a physical impossibility it will not result in a conviction for attempt. If, however, the accused intends to commit an offence and fails to succeed in his endeavour due to his own ineptitude, he will not be able to rely on the defence of impossibility.

It would appear that abandonment is not a defence to a charge of attempt on the basis that the offence is committed where the accused intends to commit the substantive offence and carries out acts sufficiently proximate to that offence.

CONSPIRACY

At common law, conspiracy occurs where two or more people enter into an agreement to commit an unlawful act, which can sometimes include civil wrongs. It is important to note that the actual offence need never be committed and an accused can still be convicted where the objective of the conspiracy is not achieved as was the case in *The People (Director of Public Prosecutions) v O'Brien*, unreported, Court of Criminal Appeal, June 17, 2002. The essence of the offence is the concluded agreement between the parties to commit an offence, a matter which can be inferred by the jury from the conduct of the accused.

The actus reus of conspiracy is the agreement *concluded* between the parties. It is essential that the agreement is more than a mere discussion of the offence. In *R v Walker* [1962] Crim. L.R. 458, it was held that no conspiracy occurs in the absence of a formal agreement between the parties to commit the substantive offence.

The mens rea is the intention to commit the substantive offence. The accused need not be aware of the precise details of the substantive offence but he must have knowledge of the nature of the intended offence. In *R v Orton* [1922] V.L.R. 469, it was held that an accused could be convicted of conspiracy even where he did not know the precise details of the offence. The court held that where the accused was aware that the activity being planned was a crime, it did not matter that he did not know all the details. A similar ruling was given in *R v Porter* [1980] N.I. 18.

Where there are a number of individuals accused of conspiring with one another, it need not be the case that each individual knew about all the others. Where someone joins in a conspiracy already hatched by others, he will also be convicted. This can be seen in the case of *Attorney General v Oldridge* [2000] 4 I.R. 593. In this case, the accused had agreed to participate in a fraudulent scheme which had already been put into operation by others.

A statutory offence of conspiracy was created by s.71 of the Criminal Justice Act 2006 which applies to conspiracy in the context of the offences governed by that Act. Accordingly, where the offence does not pertain to criminal organisations, the common law offence of conspiracy applies.

IMPOSSIBILITY

If the agreement entered into relates to a specific endeavour which is impossible to achieve, no conviction will follow. In *DPP v Nock* [1978] 2 All E.R. 654, the defendants were charged with conspiring to produce cocaine. Unknown to the accused, the material with which he was working did not contain any cocaine and consequently he could not have produced the drug. The convictions for conspiracy were quashed by the House of Lords where it was held that where the agreement between the defendants was to achieve a specific result and where that result was an impossibility, the defendants could not be convicted. The House of Lords also pointed out that where the indictment was drafted in very specific terms, no conviction could result. Where the indictment was drafted in more general terms, the court held that a conviction could be possible.

Where a party to a conspiracy subsequently pulls out of the agreement, this may amount to a mitigating factor. It would seem that a conviction could still be forthcoming since the withdrawal from the agreement is dependant on being part of the agreement to begin with.

INCITEMENT

Incitement occurs where the accused persuades or influences another person to commit an offence or where a person is induced to commit an offence as a result of duress exerted by the accused. In *R v Fitzmaurice* [1983] 1 All E.R. 189 it was held that incitement could be by a suggestion, proposal or the promise of a reward. In *RRB v Applin* [1974] 2 W.L.R. 541 the court held that incitement can also occur where the accused uses threats to induce a person to commit a crime.

The actus reus of incitement is persuading another person, by whatever means, to engage in the commission of an offence. In this way it is similar to solicitation. The leading Irish case on incitement is *The People (Attorney General) v Capaldi* [1949] 1 Frewen 95. The defendant enquired of a doctor whether something could "be done" for a pregnant woman. Implicit in the enquiry was the doctor's willingness to perform an abortion. The doctor was also assured that money was no object, whereupon the doctor refused and asked the defendant to leave the surgery. The accused was convicted of incitement and appealed. The Court of Criminal Appeal held that incitement involved more than the mere expression of a desire. However, in this case the defendant had gone further than simply articulating a desire and had offered a financial incentive. On that basis, the court upheld his conviction for incitement.

The incitement must be communicated either to a specific person or to a group of people. The accused can be prosecuted for attempted incitement where the communication fails for some reason. Additionally, where a person incites another to commit an offence and that other person agrees, both can then be charged with conspiracy. It had been the case that where the person being incited by the accused was deemed incapable of committing a criminal offence by reason of *doli incapax*, the accused could not be convicted of incitement. This is arguably no longer the case by virtue of the changes brought about by the Criminal Justice Act 2006 in respect of the criminal liability of children.

The mens rea for incitement is intention. The accused must intend that the person being incited will commit the offence. Therefore, there can be no incitement if the accused knows that the incitee lacks the legal capacity to commit the offence. In *R v Whitehouse* [1977] 3 All E.R. 737 the accused was charged with incitement to commit incest. The incitee was his 15-year-old daughter. Since the offence of incest by a female could only be committed by a female above the age of 16, the accused could not be convicted of incitement.

IMPOSSIBILITY

The defence of impossibility operates in much the same way with regard to incitement as it does to the other inchoate offences and its success will depend on whether the incitement relates to a specific type of act or a more general one. Impossibility may be a defence in the former, but will not be a defence in the latter. It should be noted that where the incitee goes further that what was actually incited, the accused will not be guilty of incitement in relation to this further offence.

PUNISHMENT ON CONVICTION

Punishment for incitement depends on whether the substantive offence is actually committed. Where the accused is charged with incitement of a summary offence which is committed the punishment is governed by s.22 of the Petty Sessions (Ireland) Act 1851. In the case of indictable offences, the punishment is provided for by s.7(1) of the Criminal Law Act 1997. Where the substantive offence is not actually committed, the matter of punishment is at the judge's discretion.

STATUTE

A statutory offence of incitement is provided for by the Prohibition of Incitement to Hatred Act 1989 which prohibits the publication, distribution or broadcast of any material that is threatening, abusive or insulting with the intention to incite hatred against a group of people or being reckless as to whether hatred is incited.

Introduction to Criminal Defences

17

In order to discharge the onus of proof, the prosecution must not only prove all the elements of the offence(s) with which the defendant is charged but also negative or disprove any and all defences and explanations that are consistent with the defendant's innocence. This is part and parcel of what was referred to as "the golden thread" in *Woolmington v DPP* [1935] A.C. 462. Criminal defences may be categorised in a number of ways. Some defences are available only to a charge of murder and are partial defences only. A partial defence is one which will result in a conviction for a lesser offence than that which the accused is charged with. In the case of Provocation and Excessive Self Defence, if successfully raised, the accused will be convicted of manslaughter, having initially been tried for murder. It is also common to categorise defences according to the rationale behind them. Some defences excuse the accused's conduct whereas others justify it. An excusatory defence effectively forgives the accused of his conduct on the basis that to punish him would amount to an injustice. A justificatory defence, on the other hand, is premised on the acceptability of the conduct of the accused. An example of the former is insanity while provocation is the clearest example of the latter.

The remaining chapters of the book deal with the defences available in Irish law to an individual facing trial for a criminal offence.

Provocation

18

The defence of provocation is one of two defences that apply only to murder, the other being excessive self-defence, which will be discussed in the chapter on self-defence. Both are partial defences and will never justify an acquittal. An accused who successfully pleads provocation to a charge of murder will be convicted of manslaughter. In the case of offences other than murder, provocation and excessive self-defence are relevant mitigating factors which may result in a lesser sentence but they are not defences per se. In order to be able to raise the plea of provocation, the trial judge must be satisfied that there is evidence of provocative conduct on the part of the deceased which might have caused the accused to lose control. If no such evidence is adduced or if the trial judge rules that it is insufficient, the defence cannot be raised before the jury.

PROVOCATION AT COMMON LAW

The common law has long regarded individuals who act in retaliation to the provocative conduct of others as being somewhat less culpable for their actions. No such allowance is made for those who act in a cold-blooded fashion. In *R v Duffy* [1949] 1 All E.R. 932, provocation was defined as "some act, or series of acts, done by the dead man to the accused, which would cause in any reasonable person, and actually causes in the accused a sudden loss of self control, rendering the accused so subject to passion as to make him or her for the moment not the master of his mind."

The common law encompasses therefore both objective and subjective elements, although the English courts have traditionally employed an objective test. The difficulties with a solely objective test can be clearly seen in *Bedder v DPP* [1954] 2 All E.R. 801, where the House of Lords rejected the argument that the particular traits of the accused should have been taken into account when deciding what the reaction of the reasonable man would have been to the provocative act. In that case, the accused was assaulted and taunted by a prostitute because he was impotent. *Bedder* was highly criticised on the basis that to ignore the particular traits of the accused and to judge him by reference to the reasonable man who did not possess the same traits was absurd. The English judiciary took a different approach in the later case of *R v Camplin* [1978] 2 All E.R. 168 and essentially held that regard should be had to those characteristics of the accused that were relevant to the case, in ascertaining whether he had acted as the reasonable man would have. The accused in *Camplin* was a 15-year-old boy who had been seriously sexually assaulted by an older man who had then laughed at him. The accused retaliated by hitting the man over the head with a pan, killing him. It is not entirely clear whether *Camplin* was decided on the basis that the decision in *Bedder* was incorrectly decided or because by the time *Camplin* had come about, s.3 of the Homicide Act 1957 had introduced a subjective element to the test into English law.

WHICH CHARACTERISTICS ARE RELEVANT?

In *Bedder*, the court rejected that the defendant's impotence was a relevant issue, clearly this would not be the position post-*Camplin* and under s.3 of the 1957 Act, in England. In *R v Newell* [1980] 71 Cr. App. Rep. 331, it was held by the Court of Appeal that for a characteristic to be relevant, it had to be something significant that set the accused apart from the general population, and that the characteristic in question had to be in some way connected to the provocation.

PROVOCATION IN IRISH LAW

The leading case on the issue of provocation in Irish law is *The People (Director of Public Prosecutions) v MacEoin* [1978] I.R. 27. Before considering the *MacEoin* decision and its impact on provocation in Irish law, three observations can be made:

(1) Given that the issue of provocation was governed by the common law, a question arises as to the constitutionality of the test laid down in *MacEoin*. The common law rule regarding provocation had not been challenged under the terms of Art.50 of Bunreacht na hÉireann and despite the number of decisions following *MacEoin* which all appear to have accepted the test formulated therein, it remains arguable that *MacEoin* is of dubious constitutionality. Notwithstanding the matter of the court's entitlement to reject the common law test, the same court in *The People (Director of Public Prosecutions) v Noonan* [1998] 2 I.R. 439 endorsed the subjective test.

(2) The decision in *MacEoin* and in particular, the test laid down by the Supreme Court in that case has been the primary basis for most, if not all of the appeals taken against convictions arising from directions given by trial judges on the application of the *MacEoin* test. This is (or should be) a clear indication that the *MacEoin* decision itself and the test laid down in it is confusing at best, if not unconstitutional.

(3) Given that provocation is a partial defence to a charge of murder only, with the consequence that the accused will be convicted of the lesser offence of manslaughter, thus leaving the issue of sentencing to the judge's discretion, the argument might be made that if the distinction between murder and manslaughter were to be removed the confusion over the application of the *MacEoin* test would be resolved. The full range of sentencing options would then be available to the judge, who could still impose a life sentence in the appropriate case.

THE PEOPLE (DIRECTOR OF PUBLIC PROSECUTIONS) v MACEOIN [1978] I.R. 27

The accused was charged with the murder of his flatmate with whom he had been a long-term friend. Prior to the killing, both men had consumed a significant amount of alcohol. The deceased, in particular, had a tendency to become aggressive while drunk. On the night of the killing, the accused returned home drunk and went to bed. He was subsequently attacked by the deceased, himself drunk. A struggle ensued, resulting in the accused losing control and hitting the deceased repeatedly with the hammer with which the deceased had initially attacked him. He was convicted of murder and appealed on the basis that he had been provoked by the deceased. The Court of Criminal Appeal rejected the common law objective test, and stated that it was no longer part of Irish law. The test, according to the Court of Criminal Appeal, was an entirely subjective one which required the jury to decide whether or not the accused had been provoked to the point where he had lost self control. Accordingly, the test for provocation was set down by the Court of Criminal Appeal in the following terms:

> "[T]he trial judge at the close of the evidence should rule on whether there is any evidence of provocation which having regard to the accused's temperament, character and circumstances, might have caused him to lose control of himself at time of the wrongful act and whether the provocation bears a reasonable relation to the amount of force used by the accused."

The requirement that the provocation bears a "reasonable relation" to the force used by the accused has led to further confusion in that it appears to introduce an objective element into what was effectively a rejection of the "reasonable man" test in the context of provocation. Subsequent cases have seen the courts attempt to explain the matter with limited success. In *The People (Director of Public Prosecutions) v Mullane*, unreported, Court of Criminal Appeal, March 11, 1997, the court decided that the inclusion of the "reasonable relation" element was not for the purpose of introducing an objective element to the *MacEoin* test but rather that:

> "[T]he impugned sentence in MacEoin really comes down to credibility of testimony rather than to any suggestion that the accused's conduct is to be once more judged by an objective standard."

This interpretation was later endorsed by the Court of Criminal Appeal in *Noonan*. In *The People (Director of Public Prosecutions) v Davis* [2001] 1 I.R. 146 the Court of Criminal Appeal commented on the difficulties presented by the *MacEoin* definition of the defence and suggested that a restatement of the defence may be required.

WHAT IS PROVOCATION POST-*MACEOIN*?

Provocation is essentially the same as it had been under the common law. Indeed, the court reiterated the definition cited above from with the objective part of that definition omitted.

MUST THE PROVOCATION BE IMMEDIATE?

The essence of the defence is a sudden and temporary loss of control on the part of the deceased. However, it appears that sudden need not necessarily be immediate, but, the greater the lapse of time between the provocative conduct and the retaliation, the more difficult it will be to sustain the defence, and may indicate revenge rather than a sudden loss of control, in which case, the defence will fail.

CUMULATIVE PROVOCATION

The issue of cumulative provocation has arisen primarily in the context of killings that occur in the context of spousal abuse. The English judiciary had initially been reluctant to accept that cumulative provocation could satisfy the requirement that the accused had to suddenly lose control due to the provocative conduct of the deceased. In *R v Ahluwalia* [1993] 4 All E.R. 88 and *R v Thornton* (No. 2) [1996] 2 All E.R. 1023, the defendants in each case had been victims of spousal abuse who had killed their husbands. In neither case did the accused react immediately to the provocative conduct. On appeal, the conviction in *Ahluwalia* was overturned, albeit on grounds other than the issue of cumulative provocation, and a fresh appeal was allowed in the case of *Thornton*. In Thornton's case the court held that "battered woman's syndrome" was a relevant factor to be considered when deciding whether the accused had been provoked. The Irish courts appear to have accepted the concept of cumulative provocation and will look at the most recent episode of provocation in the overall context of a longer period of abuse. Following *MacEoin*, it would appear that where the accused is the victim of long-term abuse, this will be a relevant consideration given the subjective nature of the test.

WHAT AMOUNTS TO PROVOCATIVE CONDUCT?

The common law referred to an act or series of acts and consequently it would appear that any act, lawful or otherwise could amount to provocation. In *R v Doughty* [1986] Crim. L.R. 625 the Court of Appeal held that a baby's crying should have been considered by the jury where the accused had been charged with the baby's murder. The defence had argued that the accused had put a pillow over the child's head in a bid to stop the child from crying. In *MacEoin*, the court referred to "wrongful acts" which could be taken to mean that the provocative conduct had to be some unlawful act. However, if the test is that of the effect of the act on the accused, there would not appear to be any logical reason to limit these acts to those that are unlawful. In *The People (Director of Public Prosecutions) v Kehoe* [1992] I.L.R.M. 481, the accused killed his former girlfriend's new partner for no apparent reason other than his presence at the house of the accused's former girlfriend. In *MacEoin*, the court also stated that words can be capable of constituting provocation.

WHO MUST PROVOKE?

At common law, the provocation must have emanated from the deceased and not from a third party. It is also the case that were the accused brings about a situation and then claims to have been provoked by the deceased, he cannot rely on the defence since the provocation was self-induced.

PROPORTIONALITY

It was stated in *MacEoin* that, "if the prosecution can prove beyond reasonable doubt that the force used was unreasonable and excessive, having regard to the provocation, the defence of provocation fails". This would appear to be a rather bizarre requirement when one considers that the essence of the defence is that of the complete loss of self-control on the part of the accused.

In *Mullane*, the Court of Criminal Appeal held that the jury might have been led to believe, from the directions given by the trial judge, that the amount of force used should be evaluated objectively and that this was wrong on the basis that the *MacEoin* test is a subjective one. A similar situation arose in *The People (Director of Public Prosecutions) v Noonan* [1998] 1 I.L.R.M. 154, where again, the jury appeared to have been directed to employ an objective test in relation to the question of proportionality. The court allowed the appeal on this basis. The subjective nature of the test in relation to the proportionality of the force used was also stated in *The People (Director of Public Prosecutions) v Bambrick* [1996] 1 I.R. 265, *The People (Director of Public Prosecutions) v Kelly* [2000] 2 I.R. 1 and *The People (Director of Public Prosecutions) v Heaney*, unreported, Court of Criminal Appeal, January 17, 2000.

KEY CASES AND LEGISLATION

R v Duffy [1949] 1 All E.R. 932—Definition of "provocation".

The People (Director of Public Prosecutions) v MacEoin [1978] I.R. 27— Leading case in Ireland.

R v Ahluwalia [1993] 4 All E.R. 88 and *R v Thornton* (No. 2) [1996] 2 All E.R. 1023—"Cumulative provocation".

Self-Defence

19

The common law has always recognised the right to use a reasonable amount of force in order to defend oneself or a close relative from attack and for the purposes of preventing the commission of a criminal offence. In *The People (Attorney General) v Keatley* [1954] I.R. 12, the Court of Criminal Appeal stated that there was no need, in this jurisdiction, to show that the accused had any special relationship with the person whom he sought to protect from attack. In general, the justifiable use of force is provided for by ss.18 and 19 of the Non-Fatal Offences Against the Person Act 1997. A question arises as to whether the common law rules in relation to self defence have been totally abolished or merely abolished within the meaning of ss.18 and 19. Section 22(1) provides that:

> The provisions of this Act have effect subject to any enactment or rule of law providing a defence, or providing lawful authority, justification or excuse for an act or omission.

Section 22(2) provides as follows:

> Notwithstanding subsection (1) any defence available under the common law in respect of the use of force within the meaning of Sections 18–19 or an act immediately preparatory to the use of force *for the purposes mentioned in Sections 18–19 is hereby abolished.* (Emphasis added).

JUSTIFIABLE USE OF FORCE

Section 18 provides that where the accused uses force for any of the reasons listed in the section, he will not be guilty of an offence provided that the amount of force used is reasonable in the circumstances as the accused believes them to be. The test, thus, is clearly stated in subjective terms but is nonetheless confirmed in s.18(5) which provides that the matter of whether the defendant was operating under one of the above grounds will be determined according to the defendant's subjective view of the situation. Section 18 also provides that "crimes" and "criminal acts" include those which would be deemed criminal even where an accused could be acquitted on grounds of automatism, duress, infancy, intoxication or insanity. The use of reasonable force is permissible in any of the following circumstances:

(a) to protect himself or herself or a member of the family of that person or another from injury, assault or detention caused by a criminal act;
(b) to protect himself or herself or (with the authority of that other) another from trespass to the person;
(c) to protect his or her property from appropriation, destruction or damage caused by a criminal act or from the trespass or infringement;
(d) to protect property belonging to another from appropriation, destruction or damage caused by a criminal act or (with the authority of that other) from trespass or infringement;
(e) to prevent crime or a breach of the peace.

The section clearly permits the use of force to protect a third party from injury, assault or detention caused by a criminal act. In doing this, the Act gives statutory expression to the common law position. In *Keatley*, the accused had been convicted of the manslaughter of a man who had attacked the accused's brother. The conviction was appealed on the grounds that the trial judge's direction to the jury had been incorrect. The Court of Criminal Appeal held that the jury should have been told that the use of force to prevent a crime was permissible provided that the amount of force used was not excessive.

The use of force to protect a third party is not permitted in some other jurisdictions unless it can be shown that there is a close relationship between the accused and the person whom he sought to protect. This can be seen in *Devlin v Armstrong* [1971] N.I. 13, where charges of incitement to riot and of breaches of public order were brought against Bernadette Devlin. Her defence argued that she had been acting in legitimate defence of herself and other residents of Derry's Bogside. The court refused to accept the defence on the grounds that there was no special relationship between the accused and those whom she had purported to defend.

At common law, a defendant who uses force in response to a mistaken belief as to the existence of a threat is entitled to be judged according to his subjective (albeit mistaken) view of the circumstances.

Section 18(7) of the Act provides that generally, a defendant will not be able to rely on the defence where he has caused or brought about a state of affairs with the intention of using force to resist its consequences. An exception to the general rule exists where the defendant is engaged in lawful conduct even where he knows that it may provoke an unlawful response from others.

Section 19(1) of the Act allows for the use of reasonable force to carry out a lawful arrest and provides that, "[t]he use of force by a person in effecting or assisting in a lawful arrest, if only such as is reasonable in the circumstances as he or she believes them to be, does not constitute an offence". Section 19(3) provides that the lawfulness or otherwise of the arrest will be judged according to the subjective view of the defendant. This allows for the defendant to be judged according to a mistaken belief.

FORCE

Section 20 of the Act defines "force" and provides that:

(a) A person uses force in relation to another person or property not only when he or she applies force to, but also where he or she causes an impact on, the body of that person or that property.
(b) a person shall be treated as using force in relation to another person if:
   (i) he or she threatens that person with its use, or
   (ii) he or she detains that person without actually using it; and
(c) a person shall be treated as using force in relation to property if he or she threatens a person with its use in relation to property.

Section 20(3) further provides that a threat of force may be reasonable although the actual use of force may not be. Where the defendant had an opportunity to retreat before resorting to the use of force, s.20(4) of the Act provides that this is a factor to be taken into account in deciding whether the use of force by the defendant was reasonable. In *R v McInnes* [1971] 3 All E.R. 295, the Court of Appeal held that while there was no absolute duty to retreat at common law, failure to do so could be taken into account in determining the reasonableness of the use of force by the accused. This ruling was approved of in this jurisdiction in *The People (Attorney General) v Dwyer* [1972] I.R. 416. The defences under ss.18 and 19 also apply to acts that are immediately preparatory to the use of force.

DEFENCE OF PROPERTY

Article 40.5 of Bunreacht na hÉireann forbids the forcible entry of a dwelling save in accordance with law. Given the constitutional protection of the dwelling the question arises as to what lawful level of force may be employed to repel an unlawful entry. Clearly, the status of the dwelling in constitutional terms and in terms of its importance to the well-being of the citizen will justify the use of greater force than could be used in repelling a threat to personal property. A further consideration arises in the context of the dwelling and that is whether a person whose dwelling is being unlawfully entered is, or even should be, obliged to retreat.

As previously noted, s.20 of the Non-Fatal Offences Against the Person Act 1997 provides that failure to retreat is a factor that must be taken into account in determining whether the force used to repel a threat was reasonable but this must be interpreted as applying solely in the context of the offences covered by that Act. The defence of the dwelling centres around the principle referred to as the "Castle Doctrine" a full analysis of which greatly exceeds the scope of this book. Put simply, the doctrine distinguishes between situations where an individual is attacked outside of his home and those in which the attack occurs in the person's home. The duty to retreat applies to the former but not to the latter on the basis that a person's home is their sanctuary. At the same time, Art.40.3.1 imposes an obligation on the State to defend as far as practicable, the personal rights of the citizen. This poses a dilemma for the courts in circumstances where lethal force is used in response to an attack arising from unlawful entry into a dwelling.

The Court of Criminal Appeal quashed a conviction for manslaughter and ordered a re-trial in the case of *The People (Director of Public Prosecutions) v Nally* [2007] 4 I.R. 145. The original conviction for manslaughter arose from the killing by the defendant of an intruder on his property. The trial judge had directed the jury that they could consider self-defence as a partial defence only and that he would accept only a verdict of murder or manslaughter in light of the excessive nature of the force used by the defendant. The Court of Criminal Appeal quashed the conviction and ordered a re-trial on the basis that the trial judge had effectively encroached upon the role of the jury.

In *The People (Director of Public Prosecutions) v Barnes* [2007] 3 I.R. 130 the Court of Criminal Appeal had cause to respond to the precise issue of the competing rights of householder and burglar. At issue in *Barnes* was whether a burglar, having entered the dwelling of the deceased could successfully invoke self-defence. The accused gave evidence that the deceased had attacked him and that he acted in self-defence. While stressing that it was not lawful in this jurisdiction to kill a burglar simply because he is a burglar, the court in *Barnes* held as follows:

(i) Every burglary in a dwelling is an act of aggression and as an aggressor, a burglar may expect to encounter retaliatory force;

(ii) In assessing whether the degree of force used in response to the burglary was lawful, the courts will apply a test comprising subjective and objective elements;

(iii) The aggressor must take his victim as he finds him and the amount of force used by the victim in response to the attack will have to be of a grossly disproportionate nature or be accompanied by actual malice before liability will attach to the victim;

(iv) Regardless of the force with which the burglar is met, he can never be seen as entirely without blame in the killing of the householder or other lawful occupant of the dwelling;

(v) Self-defence must be available as a defence to the burglar but because of his "initial, grave aggression", the killing of a householder in the course of a burglary can never amount to anything less than manslaughter.

At present there is no statutory basis for the use of lethal force in the defence of one's dwelling although it is likely that legislative reform of this area of law will take place shortly. At the time of writing, the ruling in *Barnes* has at least two important implications in the context of self-defence. Firstly, it raises the status of the defence as it applies to the use of force to repel an attack within the dwelling by linking it to the respective constitutional rights of the householder and the intruder and in so doing, incorporates the "Castle Doctrine" into Irish law. Secondly, it appears to have created a species of self-defence arising from what might be termed "self-generated necessity" whereby a burglar faced with disproportionate force in response to his "initial, grave aggression" may use force in defending himself.

EXCESSIVE SELF-DEFENCE

Like the defence of provocation, excessive self-defence is a partial defence to murder only and, if successfully pleaded, will reduce murder to manslaughter. It may be a mitigating factor in respect of other offences, resulting in a lesser sentence, but is not a defence per se.

WHAT AMOUNTS TO EXCESSIVE SELF-DEFENCE?

Excessive self-defence occurs where the accused uses more force than is objectively necessary, but which the accused believed was necessary. Where the accused used no more force than he honestly believed was necessary, he is entitled to be acquitted of murder. The onus is on the prosecution to prove that the accused knew he was using a dispro - portionate amount of force. In *The People (Attorney General) v Commane* [1975] 1 Frewen 400, the Court of Criminal Appeal upheld the conviction for murder of a defendant who used force knowing it to be excessive in the circumstances. The accused had been attacked by the deceased and had struck the deceased in self-defence. Having knocked the deceased unconscious, the accused then strangled him.

In *The People (Attorney General) v Dwyer* [1972] I.R. 416 the accused stabbed the deceased in the course of a brawl. He claimed that he did so because he believed that the deceased had a knife and was, consequently, afraid for his life. The Supreme Court held that the accused's subjective belief was sufficient to reduce the offence form murder to manslaughter.

The position in English law is different and in that jurisdiction, excessive self-defence will not reduce murder to manslaughter but may go towards mitigation of sentence. The House of Lords held in *R v Clegg* [1995] 1 All E.R. 334 that a British soldier who had shot and killed a passenger in a car which had driven through a checkpoint in Belfast, could not argue excessive self-defence when he was charged with the murder. His defence had been that he had fired four bullets at the passing car in order to defend a colleague who was standing nearby and that excessive self-defence should be accepted on that basis. Forensic evidence revealed that the fatal bullet had been fired after the car had passed the soldiers, and the defendant was convicted.

KEY CASES AND LEGISLATION

The People (Director of Public Prosecutions) v Nally [2007] 4 I.R. 145 and *The People (Director of Public Prosecutions) v Barnes* [2007] 3 I.R. 130—Defence of property.

The People (Attorney General) v Commane [1975] 1 Frewen 400 and *The People (Attorney General) v Dwyer* [1972] I.R. 416—Excessive self-defence.

Intoxication

20

There is no general defence of intoxication at common law. Indeed, it is arguable that it is not a defence at all on the basis that it might more accurately be described as evidence of the lack of ability on the part of the accused to form mens rea and it is invariably the case that where intoxication is raised by the defence, it is done for the purpose of establishing that due to intoxication, the accused lacked capacity to form mens rea. At the outset, it should be stressed that intoxication is *not* the same as drunkenness. Whereas the former may well have a bearing on liability, if it can be shown to have deprived the accused of the capacity to form the required intent for the offence with which he is charged, the latter will, almost invariably be regarded as an aggravating factor with the consequent implications as regards sentencing.

The rationale behind the defence is based on a mixture of principle and policy. It is not desirable that a person could be convicted of an offence where he could not have formed the intention to commit it. Equally, it is accepted that the public should be afforded some form of protection against the actions of those who become so intoxicated as to pose a threat through criminal activity. The defence of intoxication, may therefore, be viewed as a form of balancing act between these two considerations. Certain limitations are imposed on the application of the defence.

DISTINCTION BETWEEN CRIMES OF BASIC/ SPECIFIC INTENT

An offence of basic intent is one which requires no more than the performance of a particular act, for example rape or assault. The mens rea of any offence of basic intent is recklessness. An offence of specific intent is one which requires an intention to bring about a particular outcome, the clearest example of a crime of specific intent, sometimes known as a result offence, is murder.

In *DPP v Beard* [1920] All E.R. 21 the House of Lords held that while drunkenness is never a defence, intoxication could be where the defendant was rendered incapable of forming the specific intent to commit the offence in question. In this case the accused had been charged with murder, which is an offence of specific intent. The issue was further considered in *DPP v Majewski* [1976] 2 All E.R. 142, which case has come to be regarded as the leading authority on intoxication. In *Majewski*, the accused had been charged with numerous counts of assault occasioning bodily harm. Prior to the incident, the accused had consumed a considerable quantity of alcohol and drugs and then sought to rely on the fact that he could not have formed mens rea due to intoxication. The House of Lords reiterated the position that at common law there was no defence of intoxication but that there were some exceptions to this general rule. The main point made by the House of Lords in *Majewski* was that where an offence was one of specific intent intoxication could be a defence if it had the effect of depriving the accused of the capacity to form mens rea. Offences of basic intent were held not to be covered by the defence on the basis that they could be committed recklessly, and since becoming intoxicated was, in itself, reckless, the defence could not apply.

The *Majewski* decision was criticised as being illogical on the basis that the distinction drawn between offences of specific and basic intent was artificial. The Lords themselves acknowledged that drawing a distinction between the two types of offence was illogical but that public policy considerations tipped the balance in favour of doing so. *Majewski* was not followed in all common law jurisdictions having been rejected by the High Court of Australia in *The Queen v O'Connor* [1980] 146 C.L.R. 64 and eventually by the Canadian Supreme Court in *R v Daviault* [1994] 3 S.C.R. 63.

VOLUNTARY/INVOLUNTARY INTOXICATION

Voluntary intoxication occurs where the accused consumes or ingests some form of intoxicant of his own volition, as occurred in *Majewski*. An intoxicant may be alcohol or may be some other form of drug. In *R v Lipman* [1970] 1 Q.B. 152, the accused had taken LSD and killed his girlfriend due to the belief that he was being attacked by snakes. This belief was caused by the hallucinogenic effects of the drug. He was convicted of manslaughter and appealed on the basis that he had no idea what he was doing and had not intended to kill the victim. The Court of Appeal upheld the conviction on the basis that manslaughter can be committed through the commission of an unlawful and dangerous act and that because it was not necessary to have specific intent, self-induced (voluntary) intoxication was not a defence.

In *R v Hardie* [1984] 3 All E.R. 848 the accused took a number of Valium tablets because he was upset about breaking up with his girlfriend. Rather than becoming calm, the accused became aggressive and ended up starting a fire in his former girlfriend's apartment. Having taken the tablets voluntarily, the question arose as to whether he could rely on the defence of intoxication. In this case the court held that the accused could not have known that the tablets could cause aggression and therefore, could not have been voluntarily intoxicated. The accused was deemed to have been involuntarily intoxicated but the court stated that had he known that the drug could have induced aggressive behaviour, the defence would not have been available.

Involuntary intoxication arises where the accused takes an intoxicating substance unwittingly. In these cases, the accused will have the defence of intoxication available even for crimes of basic intent. In *R v Allen* [1988] Crim. L.R. 698, it was held that the defence is not available if the accused knows that the substance is an intoxicant, but is unaware of its potency. The defence is not available in cases where intent is not actually negatived. Most, if not all intoxicating substances lower inhibitions. Consequently, where the accused has formed the intent to commit an offence, albeit because his inhibitions were reduced due to the consumption of an intoxicant, the defence will not be available on the basis that, according to the court in *R v Kingston* [1994] 3 All E.R. 353, "a drugged intent is still an intent".

DUTCH COURAGE

Intoxication will not be a defence where the accused has taken alcohol or drugs in order to give him the courage to carry out an offence. In *AG for Northern Ireland v Gallagher* [1961] 3 All E.R. 299, the accused, having formed the intention to kill his wife, consumed a considerable amount of alcohol in order to give him the courage to do so. He then argued that he had been intoxicated to such an extent that he lacked capacity to form the required intention, and that even though he had formed such an intent earlier, the mens rea and the actus reus did not coincide at the time of the killing. His conviction for murder was upheld by the House of Lords, where it was held that intoxication was not available as a defence in a case of Dutch courage and that the killing could be viewed as a continuing act, the mens rea still being operative at the time of the killing.

INTOXICATION IN IRISH LAW

Until recently, it was unclear whether the *Majewski* decision had any application in this jurisdiction. The issue of intoxication has not been raised very frequently before the Irish courts. In *The People (Attorney General) v Manning* [1953] 89 I.L.T.R. 155 the court stated that the effect of drink had to go much further than to lower the accused's inhibitions. It also appears that the court in *Manning* drew a distinction between crimes of specific and basic intent, and stated that in terms of a defence to murder, intoxication would only have the effect of reducing the charge to one of manslaughter. Similarly in *The*

People (Director of Public Prosecutions) v McBride [1997] I.L.R.M. 233, the Court of Criminal Appeal seemed to accept the principle that intoxication could be relevant in terms of the accused's ability to form mens rea.

The question of whether *Majewski* is applicable in this jurisdiction has now been answered in the affirmative by the Court of Criminal Appeal in *The People (Director of Public Prosecutions) v John Reilly* [2004] IECCA 10.

In this case the accused was charged with murder and argued that he was intoxicated to the extent that he could not have formed the mens rea for the offence. No dispute arose over the fact that the accused remembered nothing of the incident, in which an infant was found dead beside the accused. The child had died from multiple stab wounds inflicted by a knife owned by, and in the possession of, the accused. On the night in question, the accused had been drinking heavily in his cousin's house, and had fallen asleep in the early hours of the morning in the sitting room. A cot of sorts had been made up for the baby using two armchairs. The child's mother got up the next morning and went to check on the child, only to discover that that he was dead. The accused was asleep on the couch with the knife nearby. He was convicted of manslaughter and appealed.

The Court of Criminal Appeal not only acknowledged the inherent illogicality of the distinction drawn between crimes of basic and specific intent in *Majewski*, but went further and stated that issues arising in the case could not be determined by pure logic. The court looked to the decision of the High Court in Australia in *The Queen v O'Connor* and to the decisions of the Canadian Supreme Court, which had initially accepted the *Majewski* ruling in *Leary v The Queen* [1977] 74 Dir (3d) 103 and in *R v Bernard* [1988] 2 S.C.R. 833, but later overruled these in *R v Daviault*. The Court of Criminal Appeal refused to follow the rulings in *O'Connor* and *Daviault* and held instead that the ruling of the trial judge, which had been based on *Majewski*, was correct. The position of intoxication in Irish law therefore is that which was laid down by the Court of Criminal Appeal in *Reilly*, which is the same as the position in England and Wales under *Majewski*.

KEY CASES AND LEGISLATION

DPP v Majewski [1976] 2 All E.R. 142—Intoxication a defence to an offence of specific intent only. *The People (Director of Public Prosecutions) v John Reilly* [2004] IECCA 10—Ruling in *Majewski* followed by Court of Criminal Appeal.

AG for Northern Ireland v Gallagher [1961] 3 All E.R. 299—Where accused ingests an intoxicant to provide him with "Dutch courage", the defence will fail.

Automatism

21

The defence of automatism overlaps in certain respects with the defences of insanity and intoxication. Insanity, as will be seen in the following chapter, if successfully invoked, will lead to the detention of the individual under the Criminal Law (Insanity) Act 2006 whereas the defence of automatism will, if successfully pleaded, result in an acquittal. The defence bears the evidential burden of laying the foundations of the defence and where this is done the burden of proof rests with the prosecution who must disprove it.

DEFINITION

The leading case on automatism is *Bratty v AG for Northern Ireland* [1961] 3 All E.R. 523, where automatism was defined as "an act done by the muscles without any control by the mind such as a spasm, a reflex action or a convulsion, or an act done whilst suffering from a concussion or whilst sleep-walking". In its most basic form, the defence of automatism arises where the accused had no control over his body. It is the involuntary nature of the actions that gives rise to the defence and the defence will fail where there is anything less than a total loss of control. This was held in *AG's Reference No. 2 of 1992* [1993] 3 W.L.R. 982 which followed the decision in *Broome v Perkins* [1987] Crim. L.R. 271.

In this jurisdiction, in *O'Brien v Parker* [1997] 2 I.L.R.M. 170 the High Court held that the defence of automatism can only succeed where the defendant suffers from a total loss of control. Where partial control is retained or is impaired, the defence will fail. *O'Brien* involved civil proceedings in which the defendant was being sued for negligence in the context of a road traffic accident. He argued that he had suffered an attack of epilepsy immediately prior to the attack but had testified to the effect that he had retained some element of control, albeit impaired, reduced or partial. Having accepted that automatism could be pleaded in civil proceedings, the High Court applied the principles set down in *Bratty and Broome v Perkins* and held that the defence required a total destruction of voluntary control on the part of the defendant.

INTERNAL AND EXTERNAL FACTORS

Where the automatic state is brought about by an internal factor, whether a physical or mental condition, it is viewed as being a disease of the mind and is consequently regarded as a form of insanity. This type of automatism is, therefore, insane automatism. In this situation the M'Naghten Rules apply, and if successful, this will lead to a verdict of "not guilty by reason of insanity" in accordance with the Criminal Law (Insanity) Act 2006.

External factors are those that occur outside the body of the accused but which cause him to respond reflexively. In this type of situation, the defence of automatism, if accepted by the jury, will result in an acquittal on the basis that the accused had no control over his actions. Where an external factor causes an internal factor it is open to the jury to find that the automatism was caused by the external factor. In this situation, much depends on the facts of any given case.

In *R v T* [1990] Crim. L.R. 607, the accused had been suffering from post-traumatic stress disorder brought about by being the victim of rape. She was charged with robbery and the court held that the issue of non-insane automatism should have been left to the jury on the basis that the post-traumatic stress disorder (internal factor) had in fact been caused by the rape (external factor).

Further confusion arises where the accused is suffering from some medical condition and commits an offence whilst in a state of automatism arising from that condition. In particular, cases involving diabetics have given rise to questions about whether the automatism is due to an internal or external factor and whether the automatism could be said to be self-induced.

SELF-INDUCED AUTOMATISM

Automatism is self-induced where an accused has brought the automatic state about due to the consumption of alcohol or other intoxicant. Where this occurs, the matter is essentially one of intoxication as was held in *R v Lipman* [1969] 3 All E.R. 410. The decision of the Court of Criminal Appeal in *The People (Director of Public Prosecutions) v John Reilly* is relevant to this issue on two grounds. First, the decision in *Reilly* is an acceptance by the Irish judiciary of the ruling in *DPP v Majewski* [1976] 2 All E.R. 142, and secondly, the defence of automatism was raised in *Reilly*. The accused had consumed a substantial quantity of alcohol and had fallen asleep. At some point during the night, a baby, sleeping on a nearby chair, was stabbed repeatedly and killed by the accused, who had no recollection of the incident. A key element of the defence's argument was that even though the accused had fallen into a deep sleep due to the consumption of alcohol, the cause of the automatism was the deep sleep and not the intoxication. It was argued that this ought to have been put to the jury and that if the jury accepted this proposition, an acquittal should have followed. In clarifying the issue for the jury the trial judge stated that:

> "[Y]ou have heard a lot of expert evidence in relation to things happening during sleep and if you do something that you have no control over, say the epileptic or the diabetic in a hypo or a hyper as the case may be, if they do something that they absolutely have no control over then they do not have criminal liability for that. You must do something by having a free choice, even a drunken free choice, to have criminal liability for it ... I left it open to you that if you find a free standing situation in which the accused had no control over his actions, then he would not be criminally liable and he would be entitled to a verdict of not guilty. But if that situation has come about because of his voluntary consumption of alcohol then you look instead to the law of intoxication."

The jury went on to convict the accused of manslaughter and the key issue for the appeal court was whether the trial judge's direction to the jury was a correct statement of the law. The Court of Criminal Appeal held that the trial judge's direction had been correct and that where the accused, at the time of the killing, had no control over himself and that his lack of control had been caused by his voluntary consumption of alcohol, the matter, thus, was to be decided on the basis of *Majewski*.

The older cases concerning diabetics are relevant to this issue also. In *R v Quick* [1973] 3 All E.R. 347, the defendant, a diabetic, had taken insulin, had then not eaten properly and had consumed too much alcohol, causing him to suffer from hypoglycaemia, a medical condition caused by having lower than normal levels of blood glucose. Whilst in this condition he assaulted the victim. His defence argued that he had been in a state of automatism. The trial judge stated that insanity was the more appropriate defence. On this basis, the accused entered a plea of guilty and subsequently appealed his conviction. It was held on appeal that his condition had been brought about due to taking insulin (an external factor) and not due to the diabetes (an internal factor). This being the case, the court held that the jury should have been given the opportunity to consider the defence of automatism. The court also held that automatism would not be a defence where the accused consumed drink or drugs or where he had done or omitted to do something, the result of which could reasonably be foreseen.

In *R v Bailey* [1983] 2 All E.R. 503, facts similar to those in *Quick* were considered by the court, the main difference here being that the accused was charged with an offence of specific, rather than basic intent. The defence argued that he lacked capacity, due to automatism, to form the necessary intent and that the defence of automatism applied even where it was self-induced. In *Bailey*, the court held that the decision in *Quick* as regards the application of the defence with regard to offences of basic intent was correct and that in such cases self-induced automatism was no defence. The court drew a distinction between situations in which the consumption of alcohol or drugs brought about an automatic state and those in which the automatic state was brought about inadvertently; the defence being unavailable for the former and available for the latter. Crucial to this matter was the foresight of the accused. The court held that the effects of insulin coupled with the effects of not eating properly might not be known to the accused and that knowledge of these could not be assured. Where the accused knew what might happen and had gone on to take a risk, he would have been reckless and could then be convicted of an offence of basic intent. Where this was not the case, and even where the accused did not eat properly after taking insulin, he would have a valid defence. The difference between the two cases appears to be that in *Bailey*, the offence was one of basic intent to which self induced automatism is not a defence whereas *Quick* involved an offence of specific intent to which it is not.

KEY CASES AND LEGISLATION

Bratty v AG for Northern Ireland [1961] 3 All E.R .523—Leading case in which "automatism" defined by court.

O'Brien v Parker [1997] 2 I.L.R.M. 170—For defence to succeed, the accused must have lost all control.

R v Lipman [1969] 3 All E.R. 410—Where automatism is the result of the voluntary consumption of an intoxicant, accused must rely on intoxication.

R v Quick [1973] 3 All E.R. 347 and *R v Bailey* [1983] 2 All E.R. 503—"Insulin Cases".

Insanity

22

The law on insanity has been given a radical overhaul with the implementation of the Criminal Law (Insanity) Act 2006 which came into effect on June 1, 2006. The 2006 Act repeals most of the old legislation governing insanity with the Criminal Lunatics Act 1800 and the Trial of Lunatics Act 1883 being repealed in their entirety. Prior to the enactment of the new legislation, the law on insanity was of relevance in two ways in the context of the criminal law. The first of these was with regard to the fitness of the accused person to stand trial and the second related to the application of the insanity defence itself. As a defence, insanity is of general application in Irish law and was, until the passing of the 2006 Act, an "all or nothing defence".

The Criminal Law (Insanity) Act 2006—Main Provisions

Section 4—Fitness to be tried

An accused cannot be tried if he is not fit to plead; to do so would be in flagrant breach of the rights of the accused to have a fair trial. Prior to the enactment of the 2006 Act, the term "fitness to plead" was used but this term has now been replaced with "fitness to be tried". Section 4(2) provides that, an accused person shall be deemed unfit to be tried if he or she is unable by reason of mental disorder to understand the nature and course of the proceedings.

The term "mental disorder" is defined in s.1 as including "mental illness, mental disability, dementia or any disease of the mind but does not include intoxication". The accused will be deemed unfit to be tried if, by reason of mental disorder, the accused is unable to do any of the following:

(i)   Plead to the charge;
(ii) Instruct counsel;
(iii) Elect for trial by jury where the offence with which he is charged is an "either-or" offence;
(iv) Make a proper defence;
(v)   In the case of a jury trial, challenge a juror to whom he may wish to object;
(vi) Understand the evidence.

The criteria laid down in s.4 regarding the test of the accused's fitness to plead are based on those laid down by the courts and particularly those outlined by the Supreme Court in *The State (Coughlan) v Minister for Justice* [1968] I.L.T.R. 177, where it was held that the question to be answered is whether the accused person has "sufficient intellect to comprehend the course of the proceedings of the trial, so as to make a proper defence, to challenge a juror to whom he may wish to object, and to understand the details of the evidence". Section 4 therefore mirrors the decision in *Coughlan* very closely.

Where the accused is deemed unfit to be tried summarily, in accordance with s.4(3), the court may, if it is satisfied on the evidence of an approved medical officer, commit the accused to a specified designated centre for care or treatment on an in-patient or out-patient basis, as appropriate. Similar provisions apply in the case of an accused charged with an indictable offence. The proceedings will then be adjourned until further order of the court. The issue of fitness to plead relates to the mental capacity of the accused *at the time of the trial—not at the time of the commission of the alleged offence.*

SECTION 5—VERDICT

Prior to the passing of the 2006 Act, the verdict in the case of an accused person who successfully invoked the insanity defence was "guilty but insane". The verdict sounded contradictory due to the use of the word "guilty" although it was held in *The People (Director of Public Prosecutions) v Gallagher* [1991] I.L.R.M. 339 to be, in fact, an acquittal. Section 5 provides that where, at the time of the commission of the alleged offence, the accused was:

(i)   Suffering from a mental disorder, and
(ii) The mental disorder was such that the accused person should not be held responsible because he did not know the nature and quality of the act or did not know that what he was doing was wrong or was unable to refrain from committing the act,

the court shall return a special verdict to the effect that the accused is "not guilty by reason of insanity". Section 5 therefore incorporates aspects of the M'Naghten rules, which will be dealt with below, and also the concept of irresistible impulse.

SECTION 6(1)—DIMINISHED RESPONSIBILITY

Where the charge against the accused is one of murder and the court finds that at the time of the killing, the accused was suffering from a mental disorder which would not justify a finding of not guilty by reason of insanity but which affected the accused in such a way as to significantly reduce his responsibility for the act, the court will find the accused not guilty of murder but guilty of manslaughter. Section 6 requires the defence to establish that:

(i)   The accused committed the alleged act;
(ii) The accused was, at that time, suffering from a mental disorder; and
(iii) The mental disorder would not justify a verdict of not guilty by reason of insanity but was sufficient to diminish the accused's responsibility for the act.

Section 6(3) provides that a woman found guilty of infanticide may be dealt with under s.6(1). Even before the passing of the 2006 Act, it is likely, following the decision in *Doyle v Wicklow County Council* [1974] I.R. 55, that an accused could rely on the defence of insanity in situations where his ability to exercise judgement was in some way diminished.

APPEALS

Sections 7 and 8 provide for appeals against findings of unfitness to be tried and against the "not guilty by reason of insanity" verdict respectively. There were no such provisions under the repealed legislation.

THE MENTAL HEALTH (CRIMINAL LAW) REVIEW BOARD

In keeping with the obligations of the European Convention on Human Rights, s.11 provides for the establishment of An Bord Athbhreithnithe Meabhair-Shláinte (An Dlí Coiriúl)/The Mental Health (Criminal Law) Review Board. The Board is an independent body with responsibilities and powers conferred on it under the 2006 Act. Those powers are set out in s.12 and include the regular review of the detention of individuals detained following the passing of the special verdict or those who are detained in designated centres following a finding of unfitness to be tried. The Review Board, in carrying out its functions, may, among other things, direct in writing the consultant psychiatrist responsible for the care and treatment of a patient whose case is being reviewed by the Board, to arrange for the patient to attend before the Board, or direct in writing any person whose evidence is required by the Board to attend before the Board to provide such evidence. Failure to comply with the directions of the Board and, further, anything done in relation to the proceedings before the Board which, if done in relation to proceedings before a court by a witness, would amount to contempt of court is an offence punishable on summary conviction by a maximum term of 12 months' imprisonment and/or a fine of €3,000.

INSANITY

The Defence of Insanity under the M'Naghten Rules

Where the accused, having been deemed fit to stand trial, wishes to raise the defence of insanity, the burden of proof shifts to him and this burden may be discharged on the civil standard of proof (i.e. on the balance of probabilities). The burden then shifts back to the prosecution who must disprove the defence beyond a reasonable doubt. The defence as it is known today emerged in *R v Hadfield* (1800) 27 St Tr 1281. The defendant believed that he had to kill himself in order to save mankind but, believing suicide to be a sin, he elected to shoot the King instead in the hope that he would be hanged. He was charged with treason, which was a capital offence.

The court held that he was insane and he was duly acquitted. The rules governing the issue of insanity were formulated by the law lords following the acquittal on grounds of insanity of the accused in *R v M'Naghten* [1843] All E.R. 229. The accused, while suffering from a delusion that he was being persecuted by the Tory Party, decided to shoot Sir Robert Peel, but shot and killed Peel's secretary instead. He was acquitted on the basis that he was insane. The subsequent public outcry prompted the House of Lords to pose a number of questions regarding the matter to the Law Lords. The responses to those questions are known as the M'Naghten Rules and are the exclusive test of insanity in English Law.

In *R v Windle* [1952] 2 All E.R. 1, the accused was convicted of the murder of his wife, believing, due to mental illness, that it was morally right to do so. The accused did, however, know that his conduct was legally wrong. He sought to rely on the defence of insanity, but was precluded from doing so because he knew that he had been acting unlawfully and consequently could not avail of the M'Naghten Rules. The court held that as far as the law in England is concerned, the defence of insanity is based entirely on the M'Naghten Rules. In Ireland, the M'Naghten Rules are the primary test but are not the "sole and exclusive test". This was held by the Supreme Court in *The People (Attorney General) v O'Brien* [1936] I.R. 236 and was upheld in *Doyle v Wicklow County Council* [1974] I.R. 55.

The M'Naghten Rules

Any discussion of the application of the M'Naghten Rules from the point of view of Irish law must proceed on the basis that first, they are *not* the sole test for insanity in Irish criminal law, although they have been the primary test, and secondly, must now be construed in light of the provisions of the 2006 Act. The M'Naghten Rules are as follows:

(1) Where the accused is suffering from a *partial delusion* but knows, despite the delusion, that his actions are unlawful, he will have no defence.

(2) Every person is presumed to be sane but this presumption is rebuttable. The presumption is rebutted on the civil standard of proof which is the balance of probabilities.

(3) The accused must show that when he committed the offence, he was suffering from a defect of reason caused by a disease of the mind, and that he didn't know the nature and quality of his actions or if he did appreciate the quality of his actions, that he did not know they were unlawful.

(4) An accused person suffering from a partial delusion should be treated as though the facts of his delusion were real.

DEFECT OF REASON FROM A DISEASE OF THE MIND

Defect of reason from a disease of the mind in this context can include conditions arising from other medical conditions. In *R v Kemp* [1957] 1 Q.B. 399, the accused attacked his wife with a hammer. He was found to have been suffering from a defect of reason from a disease of the mind brought on by arteriosclerosis, a medical condition which had caused congestion of blood in his brain. In *Ellis v Director of Public Prosecutions* [1990] 2 I.R. 291, the accused was charged with murder and sought to rely on the defence of automatism on the basis that he was suffering from the effects of epilepsy at the time of the killing. The judge directed the jury to disregard the issue of automatism and to consider the issue of insanity. The accused was found to be guilty but insane.

In *R v Quick* [1973] 3 All E.R. 347, the defendant was a diabetic, who neglected to follow medical advice in relation to his condition. While suffering from hypoglycaemia as a result, he committed an assault. He argued that he should be acquitted on the basis of automatism but the trial judge directed that his defence was that of insanity. On that basis he entered a plea of guilty and subsequently appealed his conviction. The Court of Appeal held that the defendant's condition had been brought about by his failure to follow medical advice. As this was an external factor, there was no disease of the mind and consequently the defendant could not avail of the defence of insanity.

In *R v Sullivan* [1983] 2 All E.R. 673, the opposite conclusion was arrived at in the case of an epileptic who committed an assault. In this case the court followed the decisions in *Kemp* and *Quick* and found that epilepsy, being an internal factor, gave rise to a defence of insanity.

The defence is not available to someone who, through lack of care or through absentmindedness, commits an offence. In *R v Clarke* [1972] 1 All E.R. 219, the accused tried to assert that forgetfulness, caused by depression had caused her to shoplift. At her trial, it was held that this could give rise to the defence but the proposition was rejected on appeal where the court held that the defence avails those who have, through a defect of reason from a disease of the mind, lost the power to reason and did not apply to those who simply failed to exercise that reason.

NATURE AND QUALITY OF THE ACT

In addition to the foregoing, the accused must also show that he either did not know the nature and quality of the act or that if he did, that he did not know it was unlawful. The lack of knowledge regarding the nature and quality or unlawfulness of the act must have been caused by the defect in reason.

In *R v Codere* (1916) 12 Cr. App. Rep. 21, a soldier was convicted of the murder of a fellow soldier. He had argued that "nature" and "quality" suggested that there were different factors to be considered in the context of insanity. "Nature", he argued referred to the physical aspect of the act while "quality" referred to its moral character. The Court of Appeal held that the belief of the accused with regard to the moral aspect of the act was of no consequence. He could still be convicted if he knew he was killing someone, regardless of what his reasons for doing so might be.

In *R v Dickie* [1984] 3 All E.R. 173, the accused knowingly started a fire. The fact that he was suffering from a manic-depressive condition at the time was held not to be relevant, what mattered was that he was aware of the nature and quality of his action.

THE WRONGFUL NATURE OF THE ACT

The accused must also have been aware of the wrongfulness of his actions. Wrongfulness in this context means unlawful. Where the accused knew that his actions were unlawful, the defence will fail. In *R v Windle* [1952] 2 All E.R. 1, the accused killed his wife by giving her an overdose. She had frequently asserted that she wished to commit suicide and there was evidence that she was insane. The court even accepted that the accused might have been suffering from a form of insanity communicated to him from his wife.

Despite this, the defence failed because the accused had stated to the police "I suppose they will hang me for this." This statement by the accused showed that he appreciated that his actions were unlawful notwithstanding the probability that he himself was suffering from some form of mental disorder.

IRRESISTIBLE IMPULSE

In English law, the issue of irresistible impulse can be viewed as a form of diminished responsibility in cases of murder only. The effect of the defence is to reduce a charge of murder to one of manslaughter. Outside of that limited situation, irresistible impulse is not covered. The M'Naghten Rules exclude the concept and this point has been made in a number of English cases. In *R v Kopsch* (1925)19 C.R. App. Rep. 50, the notion that the accused could not prevent himself from strangling his aunt was described as "a fantastic and subversive theory". The point was made in even starker terms in *R v Creighton* (1909) 14 CCC 349, where the accused was informed that, "if you cannot resist an impulse in any other way, we will hang a rope in front of your eyes, and perhaps that will help".

The Irish position on the matter is different. As stated previously, the M'Naghten Rules are *not* the sole and exclusive test of insanity in this jurisdiction and in the context of irresistible impulse, the Irish judiciary have accepted that this can be viewed as a form of insanity. This has now been put on a statutory footing in s.5(1)(b)(iii) of the 2006 Act which expressly provides for the concept of irresistible impulse. In *The People (Attorney General) v Hayes*, unreported, Court of Criminal Appeal, November 30, 1967, the Court of Criminal Appeal held that in the case of an accused person who had killed his wife in circumstances where he could not stop himself from doing so, the defence of insanity should be available, notwithstanding the fact that the accused was aware of the nature and quality of his actions and knew they were wrong, but was unable to prevent himself from committing them due to a defect of reason caused by a disease of the mind. In *Doyle v Wicklow County Council* [1974] I.R. 55, the Supreme Court reiterated this position. In *The People (Attorney General) v McGrath* [1960] 1 Frewen 267 the Court of Criminal Appeal rejected the argument that a conviction ought to be overturned on the grounds that the accused was acting under an irresistible impulse. Although the appeal failed, it was not because the court would not accept that irresistible impulse was a form of insanity, but rather because there was no evidence to support the claim that the accused had in fact been suffering from it. In *Hayes*, Henchy J. held that the defence of insanity could not be denied to an accused where, due to an irresistible impulse, caused by mental illness, the accused had killed his wife. This was upheld in Doyle, where the Supreme Court held that it would be unjust to deny the defence of insanity in the case of an accused who, suffering from mental illness, was unable to resist the impulse to burn down an abattoir.

THE CONSEQUENCES OF THE PLEA OF INSANITY

In *The People (Director of Public Prosecutions) v Gallagher* [1991] I.L.R.M. 339, the Supreme Court held that the verdict of "guilty but insane" was, in fact, an acquittal. Prior to the passing of the 2006 Act, an individual found guilty but insane was detained under s.2(2) of the Trial of Lunatics Act 1883, "during the government's pleasure".

The defendant in *Gallagher* sought release from detention on the grounds that he had recovered from his insanity, but was unsuccessful. He eventually absconded and left the jurisdiction. Extradition proceedings were initiated but were unsuccessful due to the fact that he had not been convicted of any offence which would have justified his extradition back to this State. He remains at large.

The Supreme Court in *Gallagher* also stated that the issue of the release of such an individual is a matter for the Executive, but that the individual so detained could apply to be released on the grounds that he was no longer insane or a danger. The Government or the relevant Minister would then be obliged to enquire into the continued detention, and the conclusion reached would not be reviewable by the courts. It would appear that the refusal to conduct such an enquiry might give rise to judicial review proceedings. It does seem odd that a person, who by definition was sane, having been deemed fit to stand trial could have been detained indefinitely (or at all) following the verdict under s.2(2) of the 1883 Act.

The 2006 Act makes provision for the detention of accused persons found not guilty by reason of insanity:

> if the court, having considered any report submitted to it … and such other evidence as may be adduced before it, is satisfied that an accused person found not guilty by reason of insanity … is suffering from a mental disorder (as defined in the Mental Health Act 2001) and is in need of in-patient care or treatment in a designated centre, the court shall commit that person to a specified designated centre until an order is made under s. 13.

This section of the 2006 Act deals with the review of detention. The fact that "mental disorder" is to be construed within the meaning of the Mental Health Act 2001 means that a person suffering from a condition such as diabetes is unlikely to find themselves detained following a verdict of not guilty by reason of insanity.

KEY CASES AND LEGISLATION

R v M'Naghten [1843] All E.R. 229—Case which led to the M'Naghten Rules.

Irish law on Insanity radically amended by the Criminal Law (Insanity) Act 2006.

The People (Attorney General) v O'Brien [1936] I.R. 236 and *Doyle v Wicklow County Council* [1974] I.R. 55—M'Naghten Rules not the sole and exclusive test of insanity in Irish law.

Duress and Necessity

23

DURESS

The defence of duress is available to an accused person who has been charged with an offence other than murder, attempted murder and treason. It applies where the accused acted as he did due to threats made against him or a third party. The threat must be of a serious nature and the duress must be operating at the time of the commission of the offence. The determining issue here is not whether the accused had formed mens rea but rather whether his will was overborne to the point where he could not be blamed for acting as he did.

The leading Irish case on duress is *The People (Attorney General) v Whelan* [1934] I.R. 518, where the accused was charged with receiving stolen money. He stated that threats of extreme violence had compelled him to act as he did. The jury agreed and the matter was referred to the Court of Criminal Appeal, which was asked whether or not, given the finding of the jury, the accused was guilty or innocent of receiving stolen property. Murnaghan J. in the Court of Criminal Appeal held that:

> "[T]hreats of immediate death or serious personal violence so great as to overbear the ordinary power of human relations should be accepted as justification for acts which would otherwise be criminal. The application of this general rule must, however, be subject to certain limitations."

The test laid down in *Whelan* appears to be *objective*, referring as it does to the "ordinary power of human resistance" and not to the power of the accused to resist. The test further requires that the threat should be immediate so that a threat to inflict injury at some future juncture will negative the defence since the accused could hardly argue that his will could be overborne to such an extent by a remote threat. *Whelan* is also accepted as authoritative in many other common law jurisdictions.

The duress must not be self-induced. In *R v Shepard* [1987] 86 Cr. App. R. 47, the accused had joined a gang who engaged in shoplifting. When he tried to break free of the gang he was subjected to intimidation. In the circumstances, the court held that the jury should have been given the opportunity to consider the effects of duress on the accused. However, a different conclusion had been reached in *R v Fitzpatrick* [1997] N.I. 20, where the accused had been charged with murder, membership of an unlawful organisation and robbery. In this case the defence of duress was not accepted and on appeal it was held that where an accused joins an unlawful organi - sation voluntarily, he cannot then assert that he was entirely free from moral culpability and as a consequence, cannot rely on the defence of duress. More recently, the House of Lords examined the law on duress as it operates in English law in *R v Hasan* [2005] 4 All E.R. 685, stating that:

(1) Adults of sound mind are ordinarily liable for crimes committed by them;
(2) Since the 14th century, a limited exception to this general rule has been recognised in respect of those who commit criminal offences against their will due to duress caused by the threats of another;
(3) The defence is one of excuse rather than justification and "is now properly to be regarded as a defence which, if established, excuses what would otherwise be criminal conduct."
(4) The defence, if not disproved by the prosecution, provides a complete exoneration of the accused. The burden of disproving the defence rests with the prosecution and is discharged on the criminal standard of proof;
(5) The defence is subject to a number of limitations:
    (i) It is not available where the offence charged is murder, attempted murder and "perhaps, some forms of treason";
    (ii) There must be a threat to cause death or serious injury;
    (iii) The threat must be directed against the accused, his immediate family or someone close to him;
(6) The relevant tests to be applied are, in general, objective in nature with reference to the reasonableness of the accused's conduct and percep-tions rather than with primary reference to the subjective perceptions of the accused;
(7) The defence applies only where the conduct of the accused has been directly caused by the threats;
(8) The accused cannot rely on the defence where he has voluntarily laid himself open to the duress;
(9) The accused must not have had any evasive action available to him which he could reasonably have been expected to take.

NECESSITY

The existence of a general defence of necessity is not universally accepted among legal scholars and jurists. Some argue that the defence is not one of general application but may arise in the context of some offences whereas others take the view that there is a general defence of necessity albeit subject to limitations. Debate also surrounds the issue of whether it is an excusatory defence or a justificatory one. Regardless of whichever view is accepted, the remainder of this chapter outlines the general principles of the defence and its application.

The defence of necessity has certain similarities to that of duress and is subject to many of the same limitations. Both defences arise in circumstances where the accused is forced to opt for one course of conduct over another where one involves the commission of a crime and the other involves grave consequences to the accused or a third party. Simply put, the defence arises where prevailing circumstances compel the accused to act in a particular way, and he elects to commit a criminal offence on the basis that it is the lesser of two evils. The crucial difference between the two defences is that the defence of duress applies where the criminal offence is committed due to a *threat* whereas the defence of necessity arises where the criminal act is committed due to the *circumstances* in which the accused finds himself. Accordingly, the defence is sometimes referred to as "duress of circumstances".

There had been reluctance on the part of the courts of England and Wales to accept that a general defence of necessity existed. In *R v Dudley and Stevens* (1884) Cox C.C. 624, the two accused were convicted of murder and sentenced to death, although the sentence was later commuted to six months' imprisonment. The defendants had been on a lifeboat for a number of weeks with two others and had killed one of the others and eaten his body. It was accepted that had they not done so, they would all have died. In their defence, it was argued that the deceased would have died anyway and that the defendants had acted out of necessity. The court held, however, that a decision such as had been made by the defendants would be one that would be made by the strongest at the expense of the weakest and that it was the function of the law to protect the weak from the strong. The accused were accordingly convicted.

The decision in *Dudley and Stevens* was later affirmed by the House of Lords in *R v Howe* [1987] 1 All E.R. 771. Later cases show a move away from this position and in *R v Pommel* [1995] 2 Cr. App. R. 607, it was held that the defence of necessity was available. In *Pommel* the accused had been charged with being in unlawful possession of a firearm. He argued that he had taken the weapon in order to prevent a murder. The court, in *Pommel* set out a number of limitations on the application of the defence which are identical to those that apply in the context of duress. The accused must have no alternative action available to him and must go no further than is necessary to avoid the greater of the two evils. Like the defence of duress, the defence of necessity may not be invoked where the accused brings about the prevailing circumstances.

In *R v Martin* [1989] 1 All E.R. 652 the Court of Appeal held that the defence of necessity was available only if, from an objective standpoint, the accused could be said to have acted reasonably and proportionately in order to avoid a threat of death or serious injury. The test for necessity laid down in *Martin* is a two-stage test with the jury being required to determine:

(a) Did the accused act as he did due to a reasonable belief that he faced death or serious physical injury if he acted otherwise?
(b) Would a sober person of reasonable firmness, sharing the characteristics of the accused have responded in the same way as the accused?

If either question is answered in the negative, the defence fails.

REFERENCES TO DURESS AND NECESSITY IN LEGISLATION

Section 18(3)(b) of the Non-Fatal Offences Against the Person Act 1997 provides for the justifiable use of force against a criminal act which occurs where a defence of duress would have been available. Similarly, a defence akin to necessity appears in s.6(2)(c) of the Criminal Justice Act 1991 as amended by s.21 of the Non-Fatal Offences Against the Person Act 1997.

KEY CASES AND LEGISLATION

The People (Attorney General) v Whelan [1934] I.R. 518—Leading Irish case on duress and accepted as authoritative in many common law jurisdictions.

R v Pommel [1995] 2 Cr. App. R. 607—Defence of necessity is available but the accused must have had no other alternative.

Mistake

24

There is no general defence of mistake per se, but the law recognises that there may be situations in which the accused ought not to be convicted of an offence where he acted under a mistaken belief as to the facts of his situation. The Latin maxim *ignorantia facti excusat; ignorantia juris non excusat* encapsulates the general rule that a mistake of fact will be excused whereas a mistake of law will not.

Where an accused acts under a mistake of the law, he will be liable for his conduct. In *The People (Director of Public Prosecutions) v Healy* [1990] 1 I.L.R.M. 313, the court stated that to allow an accused to be absolved of liability on the basis that he had made a mistake of law would be "to put a premium on ignorance".

At common law, an unreasonable mistake would not absolve an accused of liability for his conduct. In *R v Tolson* (1889) 23 Q.B.D. 706, the accused married a man believing that her husband was dead, and was charged with bigamy when it transpired some years later that her husband was in fact alive. She was acquitted on the basis that she had made a reasonable mistake. In *DPP v Morgan* [1975] 2 All E.R. 347, the House of Lords held that a genuinely held belief, regardless of how unreasonable it might have been, meant that the defendants could not have formed the mens rea for the offence with which they were charged, which in their case was rape. In *R v Kimber* [1983] 3 All E.R. 316, it was held that a genuine mistake of fact could lead to an acquittal in cases other than rape. The accused will in most cases be judged according to his mistaken belief but the court must have regard to the presence or absence of reasonable grounds for the belief. An example of this may be seen in s.2(2) of the Criminal Law (Rape) Act 1981 which provides that in considering whether the accused believed that the complainant had consented to sexual intercourse, the jury is to have regard, in conjunction with other relevant matters, to the presence or absence of reasonable grounds for such a belief.

Mistake of fact will not always lead to an acquittal. Where an offence is one of absolute liability, mistake is irrelevant since no mens rea is required, proof of actus reus being sufficient to impose liability.

Consent

25

Whether consent is a defence to a criminal charge depends on the nature of the charge and the capacity of the person from whom consent is sought, to give consent. The actus reus of some offences such as assault and theft involves the absence of consent and in these situations, the presence of consent will be a defence.

Consent is irrelevant for other offences. An accused charged with an offence under s.2 of the Criminal Law (Sexual Offences) Act 2006 will be convicted notwithstanding the fact that the person with whom he had sexual intercourse purported to consent to it, unless he had genuinely believed that the person was over the age of consent. Equally, an accused who ends another person's life, even at that other person's request and with their consent, will still be convicted of murder.

Index